"Playing Up Again"

Behaviour Scripts for
School Assembly

By David J. Allaway

BA, Cert Ed; Grad dip (Ed Couns.)

www.behaviouruk.com

BehaviourUK
Promoting Good Discipline & Better Behaviour

Published in Great Britain by:
Behaviour UK Ltd.
PO Box 59
Cowbridge
CF71 9AN

www.behaviouruk.com

Printed in Great Britain by:
The Cromwell Press Ltd
Trowbridge
Wiltshire

A catalogue record of this book is available from the British Library

ISBN: (thirteen)   978-0-9553517-7-8

Some of the National Curriculum Objectives of PSHE/Citizenship as satisfied in these play scripts

- Why and how rules and laws are made and enforced; why different rules are needed in different situations and how to take part in making and changing rules.

- To realise the consequences of anti-social and aggressive behaviour, such as bullying and racism, on individuals and communities.

- To see that there are different kinds of responsibilities, rights and duties at home, at school and in the community and that these can sometimes conflict with each other.

- To reflect on spiritual, moral, social and cultural issues, using imagination to understand other people's experiences.

- To resolve differences by looking at alternatives, making decisions and explaining choices.

- To resist the pressure to do wrong.

- Make real choices and decisions.

- Develop respect for the value and uniqueness of others.

- Exploring both common ground and differences in lifestyle and norms of behaviour among their peers, in the local community and in wider society.

- To recognised that goodwill is essential to positive and constructive relationships.

- To negotiate within relationships, recognising that actions have consequences and when and how to make compromises.

Possible ways to use these scripts:

- The material is able to be **photocopied** within the purchasing school and so teachers may wish to delete the names of some of the characters before photocopying and replace them with other **names, more common in their own region.**

- Teachers may wish to use the **preliminary questions** with their classes as an introduction to the topic before reading the play itself.

- The short plays are designed to be **read/acted out in Assemblies,** form/class periods, senior circle time or with small groups of pupils within a pupil support centre. They could also be used **in classrooms** within a lesson for subjects such as PSHE, Citizenship or English.

- There are plenty of acting parts available. This can enable many pupils to take on a short role or pupils can **double up** by reading a number of parts.

- Each play's final scene takes the form of a radio phone-in which helps to show pupils how the public outside of school has thoughts to offer about that topic. *Some pupils may even wish to phone a radio phone-in later and give their own views on issues. Teachers could ask them to tape their contribution and be given an oral assessment on how they coped.*

- Each scene comes with its own follow-up questions. These can either be tackled at the end of each scene or all together at the end of the play.

- Some teachers may also wish to ask characters questions by asking pupils to **respond in character** as if they were that person.

Useful phrases and expressions that older pupils may find useful when responding to questions:

- ❖ "On the one hand I . . . but on the other hand . . ."

- ❖ "I used to . . . whereas now I . . ."

- ❖ "I personally feel that this character . . ."

- ❖ "I accept that . . . but it's also worth considering whether . . ."

- ❖ "I understand your point but have you considered . . .?"

Index of the plays and topics:

1. "Tools For The Job"

This looks at why people need to bring the right equipment/tools to do their job. This includes bringing the right equipment to lessons *(15 possible acting parts)*

2. "I Said Look This Way!"

This looks at some of the behaviours that can make learning difficult in a classroom. These include: rocking back on chairs; calling out in class; putting down the views of others and barging into the room *(12 possible acting parts)*

3. "Let's Not Talk To Her Anymore"

This focuses on bullying and how some pupils choose to be cruel or unkind to others. It looks at how it can affect them, their family and their home life *(11 possible acting parts)*

4. "Leave It At Home"

This looks at the problems that can be caused when pupils bring certain items into school. It can lead to damage, theft, jealousy and negative influences on younger pupils *(16 possible acting parts)*

5. "Let's Skip Lessons Today"

This looks at the problems and difficulties that can occur if pupils decide not to turn up to lessons during the school day *(11 possible acting parts)*

6. "It's Making Me Angry!"

Looking at ways to reduce or control our anger in situations when we get annoyed. It looks at the effects of violence and anger and how it might be reduced *(12 possible acting parts)*

7. "The Public Is Watching You"

Focusing on behaviour that can spoil a school trip or excursion. It looks at the views of the pupils, staff and the public *(14 possible acting parts)*

8. "Late Again?"

Looking at the effects of lateness to class and how it can lead to problems later in life such as lateness to work or missing appointments *(20 possible acting parts)*

9. "Turn Off That Mobile!"

Looking at the benefits and the problems created by pupils using mobile phones *(13 possible acting parts)*

10. "I'm Telling You For Your Own Safety"

This looks at the problems caused when pupils fail to listen to instructions given for their own safety and the safety of others *(15 possible acting parts)*

Preface from the writer:

Having taught English in a variety of schools in both Britain and Australia, I was always looking for different "formats" for my lessons and Assemblies to keep the pupils interested and on their toes.

As a Pastoral Head/Head of Year, I was also constantly on the look out for ways to make pupils aware of their behaviour and how they were coming across to others by their choice of actions.

Some of you may use my original "Detention Papers" or "Interactive Conduct File" material with individual pupils. I also wanted to produce a booklet of plays/scripts based on behaviour incidents that whole classes or Assemblies could use. It's a great format as pupils love reading the spoken parts in lessons or Assemblies.

I wanted to keep the plays relatively brief so that questions could also be addressed within a single lesson.

Each play ends with a radio phone-in format. I wanted the pupils to realise that the public "out there" is interested in behaviour issues in schools and has something to say. Pupils should be aware that behaviour does not stop outside the walls of their classroom!

I do hope my play scripts will provoke interest and discussion from your pupils about behavioural issues relevant to them. Ideal for school Assemblies I believe.

Also available by the same author:

"Playing Up"

Ten short play scripts with behavioural themes ideal for Junior School Assembly

"The School Detention Papers"

Photocopiable detention or behaviour support worksheets.
Versions for both secondary pupils and also for upper juniors (3 volumes of each).

"The Interactive Conduct File"

Interactive software. Versions for both upper junior and secondary pupils.

www.behaviouruk.com

www.conductfile.com

"Playing Up" Feelings Bank:

Words to help pupils describe how a character feels

A
Afraid
Agitated
Alive
Angry
Anxious
Ashamed
Astounded
Aggressive
Alarmed
Alone
Annoyed
Appreciative
Astonished
Awkward
B
Betrayed
Brave
Beaten
Bitter
Broken-hearted
C
Concerned
Confused
Cross
Cynical
Confident
Co-operative
D
Deflated
Determined
Devastated
Discarded
Dismayed
Distressed
Defiant
Depressed
Disappointed
Disgusted
Dissatisfied
E
Empty
Excited
Embarrassed
Envious
Excluded
F
Fed up
Fortunate
Frustrated
Foolish
Frightened
G

Guilty
Grateful
H
Harassed
Hopeful
Hostile
Happy
Helpless
Hopeless
Hounded
I
Impatient
Incapable
Inconvenienced
Insulted
Irritated
Irritable
Important
Insecure
Intimidated
Isolated
J
Jealous
L
Let down
Low
Lonely
Lucky
Left out
Liked
M
Misunderstood
Mixed up
Miserable
Motivated
Muddled
N
Negative
Nervous
O
Offended
P
Petrified
Positive
Pathetic
Powerless
Pressured
Provoked
R
Regretful
Relaxed
Resentful
Rejected

Relieved
S
Satisfied
Shaken
Shy
Special
Stressed
Surprised
Saddened
Scared
Shocked
Sorry
Staggered
Stunned
Sympathetic
T
Tearful
Tenacious
Terrible
Terrified
Thankful
Thoughtless
Tormented
Tough
Tempted
Tense
Terrific
Testy
Thoughtful
Tired
Touchy
U
Unclear
Unimportant
Unlucky
Unsympathetic
Upset
Useless
Uncertain
Unhappy
Unloved
Unsure
Unwanted
Used
V
Vulnerable
Victimised
W
Worried
Wanted
Warm
Worthless

Playing Up Again

Script 1

"Tools For The Job"

"Tools For The Job" looks at why people need to bring the right equipment/kit/tools to do their job.

This includes bringing the right equipment to lessons.

Actors/cast required for playscript 1

This play has (12) reading parts.

After each scene there are a number of questions to answer.

- Your teacher may decide that you should write down your answers instead of answering them aloud in class.

- Your teacher may decide that you should read the play right through first and then read it a second time, but this time answering the questions at the end of each scene before continuing.

- Decide who is to play each part.

- If you are chosen to play the part, think about how you will play the character and the voice/accent you might use.

- Will you be sulky? Enthusiastic? Sarcastic? Think of the tone of voice you might use.

- If you are performing it in front of the class or in Assembly, what might you be doing? Where might you be standing or sitting?

Cast: Played by:

Sid   (Year 9 boy)   ....

Sid's Mum   ....

Hazir   (Year 9 boy)   ....

Hazir's Mum   ....

Debs   (Year 9 girl)   ....

Miss Patel   (Home Economics
                 Teacher)   ....

Syreta   (Year 9 girl)   ....

George   (PE Teacher)   ....

Robbo   (English Teacher)   ....

Don Ratty   (Radio Phone-in Host) ....

Madge   (83-year-old lady
                 telephone caller)   ....

Krishnan   (Male telephone caller) ....

SCENE 1 – *At Sid's home. Early morning before school*

Mum: Are you coming down, Sid? You'll be late if you don't hurry up.

Sid: OK, I'm coming. I'm here already.

Mum: You're running a bit late, love, that's all. Don't want you to get into trouble.

Sid: It's fine, mum. The bus isn't due for another twenty minutes.

Mum: Have you got everything packed that you need for school?

Sid: I put it all in my bag last night as usual: pens, rubber, ruler, books, my PE gear. Everything. Stop worrying. I've got to call in to my gran's on the way. She's got some stuff for me for home economics today.

Mum: Why, what do you need to take?

Sid: Miss Patel wants us to bring some fresh fruit or vegetables this week. Gran said she can let me have some strawberries and a few pears.

Mum: OK, well hurry up and finish your breakfast.

Sid: Stop fussing, mum. I've got it all organised! I've got to go . . .

SCENE 2 – *At Hazir's home. Early morning before school*

Mum: Are you coming down, Hazir? You'll be late if you don't hurry up.

Hazir: Hang on. I just want to watch this on TV

Mum: You're running a bit late, love, that's all. Don't want you to get into trouble.

Hazir: It's fine, mum. Don't worry. The bus will wait. You should see this. Come and look.

Mum: Have you got everything packed that you need for school?

Hazir: *(Still glued to the television)* Hey! Look what he's doing now! I can't believe this guy.

Mum: What do you need to take?

Hazir: Huh? Oh, mum, don't worry about it. Hey, I can't wait to get one of those! Come and watch this . . .

Mum: OK, well hurry up and finish your breakfast.

Sid: Stop fussing, mum. I've got it all organised! What is he doing now? It's his second attempt. He'll never do it . . .

(In no hurry, he continues to stare at the television.)

SCENE 3 – *Pupils at the door waiting for the Home Economics teacher to arrive*

Debs: Well, she said last lesson we could bring anything as long as it was fresh and wouldn't melt.

Syreta: Yeah. One of the boys brought a tub of ice cream and it was melting all over the bus seat this morning.

Debs: I'll bet the bus driver liked that!

Syreta: Oh well. My mum said I could have some of the vegetables she had in the freezer.

(Sid approaches)

Sid: All right? What have you brought for Home Ec? My gran gave me some fresh pears and these strawberries. Thing is I ate half the strawberries on the way to school and my mate nicked most of the pears. If it's food you have to nail it down or he scoffs it!

(Home Economics teacher, Miss Patel approaches)

Miss Patel: All right everyone? Good morning Syreta. I see you've relieved the local greengrocer of most of his stock! Sid, are you coming down with a nasty disease or are those red stains around your mouth something you'd rather not talk about?

(Others snigger. Sid wipes his mouth.)

Come on, let's go in and see what recipes we can conjure up.

Sid: *(mutters to himself)* Hmph! She's the one with the disease.

Miss Patel: Did you say something, Sid?

Sid:	No, Miss. I was just saying how strawberries can leave a nasty stain if you're not careful.
Miss Patel:	Yes, well let's get on. Right everyone, last lesson I asked you all to bring some fresh produce and to remember to bring your gloves. Girls, I hope you've remembered to bring a clip or something to tie back your hair? Oh, and any boys with long hair had better do the same!
Debs:	Don't worry, Miss, we did.
Miss Patel:	Come on, Hazir. Let's see what you've brought in for the lesson. Then we can start preparing our meals.
Hazir:	I wasn't able to bring anything, Miss.
Sid:	His mum used the last bit of food for his breakfast, Miss.

(Hazir grimaces at Sid)

Miss Patel:	Well, Hazir, I did remind everyone to bring in some fresh produce this week. How can you take part fully in the lesson if you haven't brought the right materials?
Hazir:	I know, Miss, I just forgot.
Syreta:	Well, you're not having any of ours. There isn't enough.
Hazir:	Don't worry, I don't want any.
Miss Patel:	Oh well, you'll have to get on with some written work instead. Carry on with the food chain diagram we started last week in your exercise book.
Hazir:	I can't, Miss, I forgot to bring my exercise book.
Miss Patel:	Well, do it on paper and stick it into your book next lesson.
Hazir:	*(He seems almost afraid to ask)* Miss, can I borrow a pen please?
Syreta:	*(sounding bored)* Miss, can we start? This is getting boring.
Miss Patel:	*(ignoring Syreta)* Hazir, Do you mean you haven't even brought a pen to the lesson? Didn't you give any thought at all to what you'd need for school today?
Hazir:	Sorry, Miss.

Sid:	My mum always gets me to put what I need for school in my bag the night before.
Syreta:	Miss, can we start chopping the vegetables?
Debs:	Shouldn't we wash them first, Miss?
Hazir:	What shall I do, Miss?
Syreta:	Nothing as usual.
Sid:	Miss, Hazir can borrow my pen if he likes.
Miss Patel:	Well, that's very kind of you, Sid, but then **you** won't have a pen and I think he's wasted enough of our time. What's your next lesson, Hazir?
Hazir:	PE, Miss. We're in the gym today.
Miss Patel:	Right, well, you might as well go and get changed ready for that and then wait quietly for your PE teacher.
Hazir:	I can't, Miss. I've forgotten to bring my PE gear. I don't think mum has washed my shorts.
Miss Patel:	It doesn't look as if you're going to achieve very much today, Hazir, does it?
Syreta:	Nothing new there then, Miss!
Hazir:	Sorry, Miss.

SCENE 4 – *Staffroom later that same day*

Miss Patel:	Oh, dear, I feel exhausted. The whole lesson was a waste of time and effort.
George:	It sounds like you've just had another successful lesson with 9E?
Miss Patel:	You must be joking! You'd think they could remember to bring the right things to the lesson. I asked them and reminded them and yet they still forgot!
George:	I had them for PE just after your lesson and Hazir didn't have any of his PE gear with him.

Robbo:	Are you talking about my friend Hazir? He wasted ten minutes of my English lesson trying to persuade someone to lend him a pen.
Miss Patel:	It just wastes so much time doesn't it? You tell them what they should bring to the lesson and yet they still forget.
George:	It's not just annoying for us. All the other kids in the class miss out too and start to get bored. It's irritating for the ones who want us to get on with some work.
Miss Patel:	Well, I don't think Hazir had even thought about today's lesson before he left home this morning.
Robbo:	My wife pins sticky note messages to my brief case or up on the refrigerator door to remind me what I need to bring into work.
George:	Exactly. We're adults and we have to bring certain kit with us to work, same as the kids do.
Miss Patel:	Yes, but try getting Hazir to bring the right kit. He just does not seem able to think ahead.
Robbo:	They're hopeless. Every one of them.
George:	Oh by the way, Robbo, just before you dash off. Did you bring that article you said I could photocopy for my 10E geography today? You said you'd bring it from home today for me.
Robbo:	Sorry, George, it must have slipped my mind.
Miss Patel:	You're as bad as the kids! What hope is there for any of us?

SCENE 5 – *Talkback Radio 102.5fm & digital*

Don Ratty:	It's twenty-one past eleven and it's a fine, mild day forecast with a high of 20 degrees. We've got the latest news at midday today with Adnan Shah but let's go back to our phone-in. We're talking this morning about bad workers you've experienced. Ever had a telephone engineer who never turned up? Has your postman delivered your letters to the wrong address? Just give me a call, Don Ratty on 777942. Let's go to the caller on line seven. Madge are you there?
Madge:	Yes I'm here, Don.
Don:	What bad experiences have you had, Madge?

Madge: Well, Don, last week the kitchen flooded.

Don: Oh, Madge, I hope you had your life jacket on.

Madge: No, seriously, Don, it wasn't a pretty sight I can tell you!

Don: Don't tell me Madge, you couldn't find your spanner and had to call a plumber.

Madge: Well, Don, I'm eighty-three years old and my knees wouldn't let me bend to get under the sink. My grandson lives too far away so, yes, I telephoned for a plumber. He was here in less than an hour.

Don: So he soon had your problem solved, did he Madge?

Madge: You must be joking, Don! He took one look at the water all over the kitchen floor and he asked me if I had some tools he could borrow. He asked if I had a spanner.

Don: Hang on, Madge. Are you telling me he turned up without any tools to fix a broken water pipe? Who is this joker?

Madge: Well, I would never recommend him to anyone else. He didn't have any tools with him and he didn't even have a pen or notebook to take down any details. I even had to lend him my pen!

Don: OK Madge. Jokers like that don't deserve work do they? Thanks for your disaster story. We have to move on. Let's go to Krishnan on line three. Hello there Krishnan.

Krishnan: Hi, Don. I enjoy your show. Keep up the good work, mate. Hey, Don, that last caller had it easy.

Don: Tell me why you think that. What's your story?

Krishnan: Well, Don, I came out of hospital last week after a serious operation. I had to have a mobile barber come to my house to cut my hair. I'm not strong enough to walk into town yet, you see?

Don: Did it go well? Did you get a good haircut?

Krishnan: I certainly did not, Don. She arrived without any scissors, no razors, no shampoo. In fact she didn't bring anything.

Don: And she called herself a mobile hairdresser? What did you think of her? Will you be phoning for her again?

Krishnan: No way! She was the most disorganised worker I'd ever met! Fancy turning up to cut someone's hair and forgetting to bring your equipment with you! I told her to leave my house. I won't be phoning her business again.

Don: OK, thanks Krishnan. We've been talking with customers who've had poor services from workers. It's 11.25 and this is the morning phone in on Talk Back Radio 102.5fm & digital. We'll be right back after this commercial break.

Introductory questions the teacher may like to ask you about this topic before you start reading/acting this playscript:

1. What equipment might the following people take to work with them?
   A plumber or carpenter . . . a GP or nurse . . .
   TV repair person . . . teacher . . .

2. What equipment do **you** have to bring to your different lessons here at school?

3. How important is it that people have the right equipment with them to do the required job?

Questions about Scenes 1 & 2:

1. Compare the two scenes at home that morning. What are the main differences in Hazir and Sid's approach to the day ahead?

2. How do the two boys' organisational skills compare?

3. Which approach is similar to your own?

4. Which approach would probably lead to a more settled and productive day at school ?

Questions about Scene 3 (the classroom scene)

1. Hazir did not bring any fresh produce for the lesson. How did his actions affect the progress of the lesson?

2. How do you think his teacher felt about the lesson?

3. How do you think the other pupils felt?

4. Why could Hazir not get on with some written work instead?

5. Why was Hazir about to encounter problems when he reached the PE lesson?

6. What tip did Sid's mother use to help her son remember what to take to school?

7. Can you think of other tips to help pupils remember to take the right kit and materials to school?

8. How do **you** remember the things you need to take to school?

9. What equipment/ kit should you take to the following lessons?
   English . . . Maths . . . PE . . . Drama . . . Any practical subject like craft/technology or home economics.

10. If a plumber, carpenter, or TV repair person turns up at a customer's home to carry out work, but forgets to bring any of the kit/materials they need, what might the customer think of them? Explain.

Instant replay 1:

Read these lines again:

Miss Patel: All right everyone? Good morning Syreta. I see you've relieved the local greengrocer of most of his stock! Sid, are you coming down with a nasty disease or are those red stains around your mouth something you'd rather not talk about?
(Others snigger. Sid wipes his mouth.)

***Miss Patel is being sarcastic to Sid.
What do you think she really feels about the marks on his face?***

Instant replay 2:

Read these lines again:
Syreta: *(sounding bored)* Miss, can we start? This is getting boring.

*** Why do you think Syreta feels like this?**

Questions about Scene 4 (The staffroom scene)

1. What do we learn about the way teachers feel about pupils not bringing the right equipment/kit with them to lessons?

2. What useful tip did Robbo's wife use to remind him what to take to work?

Questions about Scene 5 (The phone-in)

1. Why were the two callers disappointed with the workers they had employed?

2. If you had been either of those two workers, what equipment/tools would you have taken with you to the job?

Playing Up Again

Script 2

"Look This Way!"

This play script looks at some of the behaviour that can make learning difficult in the classroom.

These include rocking back on chairs, calling out in class, putting down the views of others and barging into the room at the start of the lesson.

Actors/cast required for playscript 2

*This play has (12) reading parts.

After each scene there are questions to answer.

- Your teacher may decide that you should write down your answers instead of answering them aloud in class.

- Your teacher may decide that you should read the play right through first and then read it a second time, but this time answering the questions at the end of each scene before continuing.

- Decide who is to play each part.

- If you are chosen to play the part, think about how you will play the character and the voice/accent you might use.

- Will you be sulky? Enthusiastic? Sarcastic? Think of the tone of voice you might use.

- If you are performing it in front of the class or in Assembly, what might you be doing? Where might you be standing or sitting?

Cast: Played by:

Mr Barker   (Teacher)   ....

Pupils *(boys)*   Hamid   ....

                    Jack Montana   ....

                    Simon   ....

Pupils *(girls)* Sue   ....

                    Tannia   ....

Parents   Mrs Montana   ....

                    Mr Montana   ....

Phone-in Host   Don Ratty   ....

Female Caller   Brenda   ....

Male callers   Sharif   ....

                    Rabbi   ....

SCENE 1 – *In the classroom*

*(Pupils rush in/barge through the door to grab their seats.
Teacher stands at his desk looking on.)*

Mr Barker: All right! Settle down. Settle down please!

(Class continues to chat with each other and ignores him.)

OK everyone! Looking this way! Face the front, Hamid!

Hamid: I am facing the front. Nobody else is though.

Mr Barker: Well, get out your books and be ready for work. We've got a lot to get through today. OK everyone! Quiet please!

(He bangs book on the desk)

I said quiet!!

(Everyone is silent and stares at him)

Jack: Are you ready to start the lesson now, sir? We didn't know if you were ready.

Mr Barker: Well that is the general idea, yes, Jack. Right I want you all facing the front and no more talking. I shouldn't have to start every lesson by shouting at you to be quiet. We've got a lot to get through and your exams are only weeks away.

Sue: We were just getting settled in, sir, and someone, who I shan't mention, wouldn't stop talking! *(stares across at Simon)*

Simon: Oh yeah and I suppose you weren't talking, Miss Perfect?

Mr Barker: All right. That's enough. Now settle down, all of you. And the way you all burst through that door just now. It's a wonder nobody was trampled to death!

Jack: *(sarcastically)* But we were in a hurry to get to your lesson, sir.

Mr Barker: I'm sure you were, Jack but I want someone to put up their hand and tell me how you all **should** enter the classroom.

Hamid: *(Does not put up his hand first)* I know sir. Quietly, sensibly and without pushing anyone.

Tannia: Yeah, like you did I suppose?

Mr Barker:	All right that's enough. Besides, I said you should put up your hand if you knew the answer. Did you put up your hand Hamid? Did you? *(Jack starts rocking on his chair)*
Hamid:	No sir. Sorry sir.
Mr Barker:	Jack! Please sit properly on your chair. You'll break the legs off if you keep rocking back and forth on it and then you'll have a bill sent to your parents to buy the school a new one.
Tannia:	How much is a new chair, sir? His dad wouldn't pay the bill anyway.
Jack:	Yes he would. What are you talking about?
Tannia:	Well, how come he went to court last week for not paying his parking fine? My mum saw his name in the local paper. Good laugh that was. Your family never pays their bills my mum said.
Mr Barker:	That's enough. Now settle down. We're wasting valuable teaching time and the lesson will be over before we even get started! Now just place the four legs of the chair firmly on the floor, Jack, and I won't have to phone for an ambulance to take you to hospital for a broken back.
Simon:	Is this a maths lesson or is it geography, sir?
Hamid:	You wouldn't even know what day it is.
Mr Barker:	Now stop that Hamid. I won't have you being unkind to one another in my lessons. And for your information, Simon, this is a geography lesson and you should all have your geography books open. Now let's get back to the work in hand. Now, think back to last lesson and who can tell me one of the causes of a thunderstorm?
Tannia:	It's rain, sir.
	(The class all start laughing at her answer)
Jack:	You're so stupid, Tannia. That's not the cause.
	(Tannia looks embarrassed)
Mr Barker:	Now stop it, all of you! I won't have you poking fun at anyone who tries their best to answer a question.
Tannia:	I shan't bother to answer any more if they're just going to make fun of me. I tried my best.
Mr Barker:	No one is going to make fun of anybody in my lessons. Is that clear, Jack?
Jack:	But she gave a stupid answer, sir!

Mr Barker:	I said is that clear?
Jack:	Yes, sir.
Mr Barker:	Everyone has the right to answer a question in my lessons without comment from anyone else. Think how you'd feel if you'd tried your best to answer and everyone just laughed at you.
Jack:	What is the right answer, sir?
Mr Barker	You mean you don't know either, Jack? Yet you were quick enough to laugh when Tannia made a good attempt to answer.
Jack:	Sorry, sir.
Mr Barker:	And another thing. You don't just call out when you want to answer a question. Are you listening Hamid? What should you do?
Hamid:	We should put up our hand first, sir.
Mr Barker:	That's right, Hamid. Why do you think you have to put up your hand first, Jack?
Jack:	Well, sir, otherwise everyone would be shouting out all at once and you wouldn't be able to hear anyone's answer.
Tannia:	And, sir, if you see who's got their hand up, you'll know who doesn't know the answer because their hand won't be up.
Mr Barker:	OK, well I'm glad we all understand that, anyway.

SCENE 2 – *At the parent/teacher meeting in the hall*

Parents have gathered in the hall to have interviews with the teachers about their child's progress at school.
Jack's mother and father are seated at a table opposite Mr Barker.

Mrs Montana:	Yes, well we were quite pleased with that aspect of his report.
Mr Montana:	Yes, Jack's marks were very satisfactory in both maths and science. We're very pleased with his marks actually.
Mr Barker:	But I thought you said you were concerned about him?
Mrs Montana:	Well, yes we are. Lots of his teachers wrote that he's not behaving himself in class. We can't accept that.

Mr Montana: He's a good lad at home and always helps his mother and we want him to do well at school, pass his exams and get a good job one day.

Mr Barker: Well, he can be a little difficult sometimes. A little lively shall we say?

Mrs Montana: Then you must punish him. He must learn to behave himself and to do what his teachers tell him.

Mr Montana: You see, Mr Barker, I want my son to know how to behave correctly so that when he's older he'll be able to mix with all sorts of people in all sorts of situations and polite company and he'll know what's expected of him.

Mrs Montana: I mean, look at this comment from his maths teacher. "Jack often rocks on his chair and makes silly comments in class." He must not behave like that.

Mr Montana: Yes, exactly. And here's one from his English teacher: "He is too keen to hear the sound of his own voice and laughs when others don't know the answer to a question."

Mr Barker: Well, yes he does do that sometimes. I've had to speak to him about that myself. It's something I really do not like.

Mrs Montana: Well exactly. You understand what we mean.

Mr Barker: It sounds as if we both want the best for Jack. I'll have another word with him on Monday and speak to him about his behaviour in class.

Mr Montana: Good, we'd like that. His mother and I will talk to him at home at the weekend as well.

Mr Barker: I think he's just starting to realise that we all have to know how to behave appropriately.

Mrs Montana: Oh yes, I agree. Last week he was travelling on the train with me after school and suddenly put his feet up on the seat opposite. Before I had a chance to correct him, the ticket inspector noticed and ordered him to put his feet down.

Mr Montana: I don't want a son of mine acting like a no hoper. He has to learn how to behave properly around other people.

Mrs Montana: We're glad he's getting good marks in his lessons but we're not happy about his classroom behaviour.

Mr Barker: No, I totally understand, Mrs Montana. We do point out to the pupils exactly how we expect them to behave but some, like Jack, do need a great deal of reminding.

Mr Montana: To us, you see, it's just as important for him to learn not to call out in class as it is for him to get above average marks.

Mr Barker: Don't worry. I'm sure Jack will be very grateful that we've had this conversation.

Mrs Montana: Oh he will. We're only trying to do the best for him, all of us, we and his teachers, aren't we?

SCENE 3 – *Talkback Radio 102.5fm & digital*

Don Ratty: It's nine minutes past ten on 102.5fm & digital. We're talking this morning about a report in this morning's papers which says that many teachers are quitting their jobs because of the dreadful behaviour by many of the kids in their classrooms. We want to hear your views of course so let's go back to the phones. Our next caller is Brenda in Swindon. Are you there Brenda?

Brenda: Yes, Don, I'm here.

Don: What do you want to tell us, Brenda?

Brenda: Don, I read that report in the paper this morning and what I don't understand is why these teachers don't throw out of the room all the badly behaved pupils. When I was a girl we were afraid of our teachers. We would never have behaved badly in class.

Don: Brenda, if the teachers threw out of the classroom all the badly behaved pupils would that really solve the problem? Where would they go anyway?

Brenda: Well, at least the other pupils would be able to get on with their work without being bothered by these idiots.

Don: OK, well, that's Brenda in Swindon. We've got to move on Brenda. It's a busy morning and the phones are running hot. Do you agree with Brenda's views? Let's go straight to line five and say good morning to Sharif. Hi Sharif.

Sharif: Good morning, Don. Well, I have to say I don't know what these teachers are moaning about. If they can't control children they shouldn't be teachers, should they?

Don: Do you think it's as simple as that, Sharif?

Sharif: Well, let me put it this way, Don. I wouldn't let my own children misbehave at home so why should they get away with it at school?

Don: I've got to ask you, did you ever misbehave at school, Sharif?

Sharif: The teachers would have hit us if we had.

Don: Are you saying that teachers should control the kids by hitting them?

Sharif: No, I'm not saying that. But they need to teach them manners.

Don: Shouldn't their parents be the ones who teach them manners?

Sharif: That's a good point you've just made, Don. They should.

Don: OK. It's the morning phone in. 777942 is the number to ring. I'm Don Ratty with you until twelve midday today and we're talking about kids' behaviour in the classroom. Has your child ever been in trouble for misbehaving in class? 777942 is the number to ring. Let's go to line 7 where Rabbi is waiting. Good morning Rabbi, I believe you're a teacher? Not in school today?

Rabbi: No, I'm on sick leave, Don.

Don: Does the behaviour of your pupils make you sick, Rabbi?

Rabbi: No, I have a bad back at the moment, Don, but their behaviour certainly could be a lot better.

Don: Really? Well, you're the teacher, Rabbi. Teach us what it's really like in the classroom. What do they get up to?

Rabbi: Well, I have to remind them constantly about not calling out in class. I tell them not to be late to class and not to barge their way through the door. I also have to keep reminding them not to put down other kids when they get an answer to a question wrong. You know, the same old stuff.

Don: Have you ever thought of leaving teaching because of your kids' poor behaviour, then?

Rabbi: I'm sure the thought has crossed my mind but I see it as part of my job to teach children how to behave acceptably. Of course there will be a couple in any class who try to push the limits of your patience but most of them will understand why I'm trying to help them behave appropriately.

Don: We've got to go to a commercial break now but that was Rabbi, a teacher, offering us all a ray of hope there. Teachers obviously care a lot and want to help their pupils grow into decent human beings. More after this break on Talkback Radio102.5fm and digital. Back soon.

Introductory questions the teacher may like to ask you about this topic before you start reading/acting this playscript:

1. What are the general rules about behaviour that operate in your classes here? What would be the most important top five classroom rules?

2. Are they the same for every class? Do you find them fair?

3. Do you find it annoying or irritating the way some pupils behave in class?

4. Are you ever distracted by other pupils' behaviour in class?

5. What action does the teacher usually take? Does it help?

6. Why do you think some pupils choose to misbehave in class?

Questions about Scene 1:

1. Why did the teacher have to keep telling the class to be quiet?

2. What was unacceptable about how the pupils entered the room?

3. Why was Hamid wrong to be rocking on his chair?

4. It takes the class a long time to settle in to the lesson. What effect will all this have on their learning?

5. How should the pupils be ready for work?

6. How did Tannia feel when Jack laughed at her attempt to answer a question?

7. Why did the teacher want them to put up their hands to answer a question?

Instant replay:

Mr Barker: All right. That's enough. Now settle down, all of you. And the way you all burst through that door just now. It's a wonder nobody was trampled to death.

Jack: But we were in a hurry to get to your lesson, sir.

Mr Barker: I'm sure you were, Jack.

What do you think Jack intends by the answer he gives?

Questions on Scene 2:

1. What do his parents think of Jack's marks?

2. What are they concerned about?

3. Why are they particularly concerned about this?

4. What are some of the things his teachers are concerned about?

5. Imagine you are writing the school report for Hamid in Scene One. What might you write about his behaviour?

6. Why had the ticket inspector been annoyed with Jack's behaviour?

7. His teacher says that Jack will be grateful they have had the conversation about his behaviour. Do you think Jack will be? Explain.

Questions on Scene 3:

1. What reasons did the newspapers give for teachers wanting to leave their jobs?

2. Would Brenda's ideas about throwing disruptive pupils out of the classroom solve the situation?

3. Give your reaction to Sharif's views.

4. What do you think of Sharif's point that parents should teach their children manners? Should this be the role of the teachers?

5. If you had been a caller on Don's Phone-In Programme, what points might you have made?

Playing Up Again

Script 3

"Let's Not Talk To Her Anymore"

This play script looks at forms of bullying and how some pupils can be cruel or unkind to each other.

It examines how it can affect pupils, their families and their homelife.

Actors/cast required for playscript 3

*This play has ⑪ reading parts.

After each scene there are a number of questions to answer.

- Your teacher may decide that you should write down your answers instead of answering them aloud in class.

- Your teacher may decide that you should read the play right through first and then read it a second time, but this time answering the questions at the end of each scene before continuing.

- Decide who is to play each part.

- If you are chosen to play the part, think about how you will play the character and the voice/ accent you might use.

- Will you be sulky? Enthusiastic? Sarcastic? Think of the tone of voice you might use.

- If you are performing it in front of the class or in assembly, what might you be doing? Where might you be standing or sitting?

Cast: Played by:

Zadie   (girl pupil)   ....

Rob   (boy pupil)   ....

Clare   (girl pupil)   ....

Najara   (boy pupil)   ....

Zadie's Mum   (Mrs Burns)   ....

Zadie's Dad   ....

Mr Tafari   (Class teacher)   ....

Don Ratty   (Phone-in host)   ....

Callers: **Kirsty** (female) ....

                   Mohammed (male)   ....

                   Vera (female)   ....

SCENE 1 – *School Corridor, Friday lunchtime*

Zadie: Hi guys. Anyone want to borrow this CD?

Rob: Did anyone hear a noise? I think I did.

Clare: I think it came from over there somewhere.
Sounded like a pathetic little squeak.

Najara: Maybe there's a mouse on the loose! Yeah, vermin!

Zadie: All right, guys? Anyone want to come down the shops after school?

Clare: There's that pathetic sounding noise again.

Najara: Kind of annoying really, isn't it?

Rob: Yeah, let's just ignore it. Come on let's go outside.

Zadie: Am I invisible now or something? Huh?

SCENE 2 – *On the bus, travelling home after school*

Clare: Where's the bell? Hey! Next stop please driver.

Zadie: Do you want to come round later, Clare? We could watch a video.

Clare: Get lost! That sounds sad. I've got more exciting things to do with my time. We're all meeting round the bowling alley later tonight.

Zadie: Oh that's great! Shall I call for you? I really love bowling.

Clare: Who said you were invited? We don't want you with us anymore. Enjoy your video. This is where I get off.

SCENE 3 – *At Zadie's house later that afternoon*

Mum: Hello, love. Good day at school?

Zadie: OK I guess.

Mum: Can you give me a hand later? I want to pop round and cook a meal for your gran. OK to give me a hand for an hour or so?

Zadie: Mum, I don't really feel like going out again tonight. Do you mind? Sorry mum. Think I'll go up to my room for a while.

Mum: You've been up there every evening this week and all last weekend. Why don't you meet up with your friends later? Clare's mum was telling me they're all going bowling tonight. I'd have thought you would have wanted to join them? You know you love ten pin bowling.

(No response from Zadie. She stands picking at a towel, saying nothing.)

Mum: Zadie are you listening to a word I'm saying? I said I thought you would want to join them at the bowling alley?

Zadie: No, I don't really feel like it. I'm bored with bowling anyway. It's stupid. I never win anyway.

Mum: What's the matter with you lately? You always seem to be by yourself. Have you had a quarrel with your friends? Go out and mix more. Don't stay up there in your room all the time.

Zadie: Oh mum, stop asking questions all the time. I'm going upstairs. I've got homework to do.

(Zadie exits. Mother stares after her)

Ten minutes later in the sitting room

Dad: Oh it's good to be back. That traffic was particularly bad in the tunnel. It's been a long day. Zadie back already?

Mum: Yes, she's gone up to her room.

Dad: Everything all right? You two haven't had a quarrel have you?

Mum: Not really. I simply asked her to try and go out and mix more with her friends. It worries me how she stays up there in her room by herself all the time. She should be out enjoying herself with her mates.

Dad: And she won't go out?

Mum: No, she's happy to just stay up there all the time. She's so quiet lately. Just keeps herself to herself. I don't know what's the matter with her. She used to be so bubbly, so happy. I think I'll have a talk with her form teacher on Monday. Something's not right. I can just tell.

SCENE 4 – *Monday morning in the classroom*

Rob: But sir, if all essays have to begin with a short introduction, wouldn't that become boring?

Clare: Yes, sir. I always start mine with a long introduction.

Mr Tafari: What do you think, Zadie?

Najara: Who cares what she thinks?

Mr Tafari: I beg your pardon, Najara. I care about what all of you think. Zadie?

Zadie: I'm not sure, sir.

Clare: There you are. She doesn't know anyway.

Mr Tafari: Excuse me. Am I missing something here? Zadie has a perfect right to answer for herself without anyone else criticising her.

Zadie: It's OK sir.

Mr Tafari: No, it's not OK. What's got into you all today?

SCENE 5 – *Interview Room*

Mr Tafari: Of course I don't mind you coming in to see me, Mrs Burns. We both have your daughter's interests at heart, don't we?

Mrs Burns: Yes, but I know how busy you must be and I'm sure it's not really important anyway. I'm sure I'm just worrying over nothing. My husband says I'm always doing that.

Mr Tafari: You say that Zadie seems quieter lately?

Mrs Burns: Yes, she just stays up in her room and never wants to go out anymore. She used to look forward to coming into school but I have a job to get her to come here at the moment. Monday mornings are particularly difficult. Something's making her unhappy and I don't know what it is. I hate to see my daughter like this.

Mr Tafari: But she's such a popular girl, isn't she?

Mrs Burns: She always has been. I haven't seen much of her friends lately.

Mr Tafari:	Would you like me to have a word with her?
Mrs Burns:	She'll only accuse me of interfering.
Mr Tafari:	Yes, but it sounds as if we may have a very unhappy young girl on our hands at the moment, don't we?
Mrs Burns:	I just wish she would talk to her father and me and tell us what's worrying her. I've never known her to be like this before.
Mr Tafari:	Yes, Mrs Burns, it sounds as if something or someone is causing her a lot of unhappiness. Thanks for coming in. Don't worry. I'll see what I can do.

SCENE 6 – *School corridor*

Clare:	. . . and she had this stupid headband on. You should have seen her!
Najara:	What a loser.
Clare:	Hey, listen. This afternoon in PE we'll have to choose teams again. Let's tell everyone not to choose her.
Najara:	Hey, that's wicked! She'll hate that.
Rob:	We certainly don't want her to play in our team, I know that.
Clare:	She's just so annoying. She came top in most of her subjects last term and was chosen as basketball captain. "Miss Perfect".

(They don't notice that Mr Tafari has approached and is now standing behind them, listening to their conversation)

Rob:	Oh well, at least now she's learning that we don't want her in our group anymore.
Najara:	I'm going to tell some kids in the lower groups not to have anything to do with her, too.
Mr Tafari:	Oh, you are, are you?
Najara:	Sir! We were just talking about a movie we saw at the weekend.
Mr Tafari:	I don't think so, Najara. Did Zadie go to this movie with you?
Clare:	We wouldn't want her with us.
Mr Tafari:	I think we had all better go and have a talk before this goes any further, don't you?

SCENE 7 – *Talkback Radio 102.5fm and digital*

Don: 20 degree high expected today with a warm breeze from the south east. You're with Don Ratty on Talkback Radio 102.5fm and digital. We're taking your calls this morning about bullying in schools. Were you ever bullied at school? Has your son or daughter ever been bullied? Give us a call and tell us your story. Vera is on line ten. Morning, Vera. Were school days the happiest days of your life?

Vera: Morning Don. I'd rather forget about them actually!

Don: Why is that?

Vera: Well, we had this boy in school who tormented everyone. He seemed to be unhappy with his own life and wanted to make all the rest of us unhappy too. He wasn't doing very well academically and his home life wasn't too good. He was in trouble with the police and was generally unhappy with his lot in life.

Don: Let me guess. He used to come into school and bully you all so you would be as unhappy as he was?

Vera: Well, that's right, Don. We were scared of him. He gave us the creeps.

Don: If you think about it, Vera, most bullies are unhappy people who want to make others miserable too. They are telling everyone that they are unhappy in their lives by wanting to hurt and bully the rest of you.

Vera: I'd never thought of it like that before, Don.

Don: We have to move on, now Vera. We've got the news coming up in a few minutes but first let's go to Mohammed on line four. What point do you want to make, Mohammed?

Mohammed: Well, Don, my son was bullied by an older boy and it affected all of us in the family. I hated watching my son become so unhappy. We had to take him to the doctors because he was having nightmares and wetting the bed. His mother was very concerned and so was I. He should have told someone earlier, much earlier. He could have told us or his teachers.

Don: I couldn't agree more, Mohammed. They have to tell an adult so the adult can do something about it.

Mohammed: When it happens to your own child, Don, you really start to see how terrible bullying really is.

Don: How did it all get sorted out, then?

Mohammed: Well, in the end, our son became so anxious and withdrawn that one of his teachers finally got him to talk to her about what was troubling him and he eventually told her who was bullying him.

Don: Good to hear it was cleared up in the end anyway. Mohammed, you have a good day. Right, well we can just about fit in a final caller before the news and that's Kirsty. Were you bullied at school, Kirsty?

Kirsty: No, Don. I was the one doing the bullying!

Don: Oh, I see. Can you tell us why you bullied the other kids?

Kirsty: It's over twenty years ago now, Don, and I've got kids of my own but I remember when I was about fourteen I tormented another girl in our class. I used to hide her books, move her bags, scribble all over her work and generally annoyed her all day long. I even tried to get the other kids to do the same to her. I know it sounds terrible.

Don: How do you feel about it now, Kirsty?

Kirsty: It's not something I'm proud of, Don. In fact, I'm really ashamed of it. If someone treated my child like I treated that girl I'd be devastated.

Don: Do you remember why you did it?

Kirsty: Looking back, I think I must have been jealous of her. She was clever at school, lived in a nice house. She had everything going for her. Everything I didn't have. I think it gave me a sense of power.

Don: Kirsty, I appreciate your call. Well, there we are. We'll be back with more calls straight after the news. This is Don Ratty talking about the things that matter to you. Join me again in just a few minutes on Talkback Radio 102.5fm and digital. The news is next . . .

Introductory questions the teacher may wish to ask before the play begins:

1. Does anyone here know of people who have been teased or bullied?
2. How do you think someone feels if they are teased or bullied?
3. If we know someone is being teased and made unhappy, what can we do? Who can we tell?
4. "Sticks and stones may break my bones but words will never hurt me." Do you agree with that?
5. Is bullying something that only happens in schools? Do adults bully each other?
6. Why do you think someone bullies or teases another person?
7. What can teachers do to help when someone is teased or bullied?
8. If a child is teased and is unhappy, how do you think it affects his or her life at home and in their family?

Questions about: Scene 1
1. What did Rob mean when he mentioned "a noise"?
2. Why did Zadie ask if she was invisible?
3. How do you think the events of this scene make Zadie feel?

Questions about: Scene 2
1. How do you think Zadie feels as Sue tells her she isn't invited?

Questions about: Scene 3
1. Why do you think Zadie wants to stay in her room?
2. What signs does her mother get that her daughter is not happy at the moment?
3. Why do you think the mother plans to see Zadie's form teacher?

Questions about: Scene 4
1. Zadie's friends continue the attacks on her in class. What forms do the attacks take?

Questions about: Scene 5
1. Do you think Zadie's mother was right to visit the school and express her concerns? Explain.
2. The form teacher says he will talk with Zadie. Is this a good thing in your view? How could it be a positive move? How could it make things worse?
3. Zadie is obviously very unhappy. Is she being bullied? What other forms can bullying take?

Questions about: Scene 6

1. Is there a clue in this scene about why Zadie is being bullied by her friends?

Instant replay:

Najara: Sir! We were just talking about a movie we saw at the weekend.

Mr Tafari: I don't think so, Najara. Did Zadie go to this movie with you?

Clare: We wouldn't want her with us.

Mr Tafari: I think we had all better go and have a talk before this.

Write down what you think the teacher may say to them.
What might be the effect of his talk with them?

3. If you were Zadie, how would you like the situation to be solved?

Questions about: Scene 7

1. Don tells Vera why he thinks bullies do what they do. What is his explanation?

2. What effect did the bullies have on Mohammed's son and their home life?

3. What finally led to Mohammed's son getting help with the problem he was having?

4. Kirsty explained why she had bullied the girl when she was younger. Why had she bullied her?

5. How do you think Kirsty would feel now if her own child was bullied at school?

Playing Up Again

Script 4

"Leave It At Home"

This play script looks at some of the problems that can be caused when pupils bring certain items into school.

It can lead to damage, theft, jealousy and negative influences on younger pupils.

Actors/cast required for playscript 4

*This play has (16) reading parts.

After each scene there are a number of questions to answer.

- Your teacher may decide that you should write down your answers instead of answering them aloud in class.
- Your teacher may decide that you should read the play right through first and then read it a second time, but this time answering the questions at the end of each scene before continuing.
- Decide who is to play each part.
- If you are chosen to play the part, think about how you will play the character and the voice/accent you might use.
- Will you be sulky? Enthusiastic? Sarcastic? Think of the tone of voice you might use.
- If you are performing it in front of the class or in assembly, what might you be doing? Where might you be standing or sitting?

Cast: Played by:

Abu   (boy pupil)   ....

Phil   (boy pupil)   ....

Mike   (boy pupil)   ....

Naresh   (girl pupil)   ....

Simon   (Naresh's Brother)   ....

Teachers   **Mr Levy**   ....

                 Bill   ....

                 Tricia   ....

                 Paul   ....

                 Mr Andrews   ....

Parents   **Mrs Singh**   ....

Phone-in Host   **Don Ratty**   ....

Callers   **Adnan**   ....

                 Philip   ....

                 Jenny   ....

                 Cheryl   ....

SCENE 1 – *In the school corridor*

(Pupils are at their lockers getting their books and bags for the next lesson.
Some are standing around chatting.
Abu notices the laptop computer that Mike takes out of his locker.)

Abu: Oh, aren't you lucky! Is that your own? I wish my parents would buy me a laptop like that.

Phil: Must have cost a fortune!

Mike: Yeah, it's not bad actually. It's got all the latest features too. I'm quite pleased with it.

Phil: Cool design, too. Great colour. I like it.

Abu: We've still got an old PC. Dad keeps it in the sitting room and we all have to share it. Blimey, Mike you're so lucky having your very own laptop.

Mike: Well, my sister's got her own, too.

Abu: Don't your parents mind you bringing it to school? Aren't they worried about it getting damaged or lost or even stolen?

Mike: I can do what I like. Mum and Dad are always out on business. They don't mind what I do.

Abu: You're so lucky. My parents want to know where I am all the time. They'd never let me do what I want.

Phil: Yeah, I know what you mean and my Mum would never let me bring something expensive like a top of the range laptop to school . . . even if we had one! I mean it just would not happen! Never in a million years.

Abu: They let me bring an old CD player into school once for the end of year party and some kid spilt her drink all over it. They went mad! Said I would never be allowed to take anything valuable to school ever again.

Mike: Oh, my parents wouldn't care if it got broken. They'd just buy me a new one.

Abu: When your parents get home tonight ask them if they'd buy one for me, as well, will you?

Mike: Yeah, nice one! They're away on business anyway. I won't see them for a few weeks. My gran's staying with us at the moment.

Phil: Is she baby sitting you?

Mike: No, of course not! It's just so she can look after my younger sister. Anyway, we'd better get going. The next lesson's about to start.

SCENE 2 – *In the classroom after the lesson*

Mr Levy: Well, when did you last see it?

Naresh: It was in my coat pocket when I hung up my coat in the changing rooms or PE.

Mr Levy: Fancy bringing a fifty pound note to school anyway! I can't believe you'd do such a thing, Naresh. Whatever were your parents thinking of to allow you to bring that sort of money to school?

Naresh: Well, Mum wanted me to get a new jacket on the way home tonight. She will kill me now!

Simon: Yes, sir. She had to bring it to school because she has to get the new jacket straight after school ends today. She hasn't got time to go back home to pick up the money first, has she?

Mr Levy: Then she should have asked me to look after the money for her until the end of the school day, shouldn't she? Shouldn't you Naresh?

Naresh: I didn't think of that, sir.

Mr Levy: It doesn't sound as if you thought about any of it, am I right? I still can't believe your parents would let you bring such a large amount of money to school.

Naresh: Well, sir, you see, they didn't exactly. *(She looks embarrassed)*

Simon   Oh, no, you are joking?

Mr Levy: Are you telling me they don't know you've got this money in school, Naresh?

Naresh: Not really. They expected me to go home first after school and collect it and then go into town to buy the jacket. I just thought I'd save time going straight there.
                (Trying to please her teacher) Then I'd be able to spend more time on your homework, sir.

Simon:	I like it! Nice try. Wouldn't want to be in your shoes when you get home tonight!
Mr Levy:	All this is very time consuming, Naresh. Look at the trouble you've now caused.
Naresh:	Sorry, sir.
Simon:	She didn't think, did she sir?
Mr Levy:	Haven't you got a lesson to go to, Simon? Your sister has to face up to what she's done and we have to try and find it.

(Simon leaves the room)

Mr Levy:	Now, are you sure you left the fifty pound note in the changing rooms before lunch?
Naresh:	Positive, sir.
Mr Levy:	OK, well, I'll have to call a special assembly of your year group. Someone must know something about this. You see all the trouble you've caused, Naresh? Next time I hope you'll think twice before you bring large amounts of money or anything valuable into school?
Naresh:	Yes, sir. I wish I'd never brought it here in the first place. My mum's going to go mad!

SCENE 3 – *The staffroom*

(Some teachers are standing around drinking coffee and photocopying work sheets.)

Bill:	When I found them, both the younger pupils were looking through the magazine outside the tuck shop.
Tricia:	Well, where did they get hold of magazines like that?
Bill:	They told me some older lads showed them pictures from the magazine outside the school gates on the way into school this morning.
Tricia:	So how did the two little ones end up bringing the magazine into school? That's what I'd like to know.
Bill:	They told me they swapped some sweets and chocolate for it!
Tricia:	You are joking?

Paul: Well, I think it's disgusting that kids can get hold of those type of magazines. Newsagents should be prosecuted if they sell them to kids. They're degrading to people, if you ask me.

Bill: I agree. I certainly wouldn't let my children bring such filth into the house.

Tricia: Do we know who the older boys were?

Bill: Afraid not. The younger ones said they didn't recognise them. They may not even go to this school.

Paul: Well, I think it's disgusting how older kids try to influence the younger ones by showing them this kind of rubbish. They think they're being clever. They're just showing off, trying to act big.

Bill: Fancy the parents of the older boys allowing them to bring such magazines into school anyway!

Tricia: Their parents probably have no idea that they even had the magazines. They'd probably be as horrified as we are.

Bill: Are the two younger kids OK?

Tricia: Oh they think it's a huge joke. Their education began before they even entered the school grounds this morning!

Paul: What do you mean? *(The other two stare at him in disbelief.)*

Paul: What? Oh I see what you mean. But I think it's disgusting. I certainly wouldn't want my children to see such magazines. Not at that age.

Tricia: Where are the magazines now? *(Paul looks a little embarrassed)*

Paul: I put them in my bag. I was going to dispose of them later.

Bill: The bin's over there, Paul.

Paul: Oh yes, so it is. Silly me.

SCENE 4 – *Outside the staffroom door*

(A parent is talking to a teacher)

Mrs Singh: What I want to know is, what is the school going to do about it?

Mr Andrews: Well, Mrs Singh, your son's CD-player should not have been brought into school in the first place.

Mrs Singh: Oh, so now it's my fault that it's broken?

Mr Andrews: I'm not saying that.

Mrs Singh: He only brought it in to show his mates his present. He's so proud of it. His Dad brought it back for him from Spain last weekend and now someone at this school has gone and damaged it already.

Mr Andrews: Well, his form teacher isn't sure at this stage what exactly happened to it. As I say, he should not have brought it into school in the first place. We do tell the pupils in assemblies that expensive items should not be brought into school.

Mrs Singh: Well, his father is going to go mad when he hears about this. What sort of destructive pupils do you have in this school anyway? The front of the player was completely smashed in.

Mr Andrews: Mrs Singh, I have spent the last two hours trying to help your son fix his CD-player and find out who is responsible for damaging it. I called a special assembly, I've interviewed some of the pupils who were playing with it earlier in the day and I really have to ask you to leave it with me at the moment as I have a lesson to take. I promise you I shall do my best.

Mrs Singh: I know you are trying very hard Mr Andrews, and I do appreciate your help of course, but who is going to pay for the damage? That's what I'd like to know.

SCENE 5 – *Talkback Radio 102.5fm and digital*

Don Ratty: This is Don Ratty. Give me a call now on 777492. This is your morning phone in on Talkback Radio 102.5fm and digital. This morning we're asking the question, "Do kids get too much too soon?" We want to hear from you. Let's go to line nine where Jenny is waiting to give us her views. Morning, Jenny.

Jenny:	Hi, Don.
Don:	Do your kids get given too much, Jenny?
Jenny:	I think we try not to spoil them, Don, but they come home from school saying, "Oh, the other kids have all got the latest whatever. Why can't we have one?"
Don:	So do you give in and buy it for them?
Jenny:	We can't afford to, Don. If they need something for school then of course we make sure they have it but some of the things these other kids get given amazes me, it really does, Don. When my kids see those things they want them too! So what can you do?
Don:	You can say no, Jenny, that's what you can do! I think some parents have lost the word "No" from their vocabulary! Right we've got to move on. The lines are running hot as usual this morning. Let's go straight to Adnan on line four and hear what he wants to tell us. Morning, Adnan.
Adnan:	Yes, hello Don. It's an interesting topic you're talking about this morning. I'm a teacher on sick leave at the moment but I spend half my school day trying to find expensive items that have been brought by the kids into school and then either lost or damaged or even stolen. I don't know where these parents get all the money from. I'm talking really expensive items that some of the kids bring into school, Don.
Don:	Why do you allow them to bring them into school, Adnan? Can't you just ban them from bringing them in? You shouldn't have to spend valuable teaching time running round interviewing kids who steal or damage expensive items that shouldn't even be in the school.
Adnan:	I agree, Don. But the parents shouldn't let their kids take such items to school in the first place!
Don:	Well, maybe we'll hear from some of the kids who can tell us why they want to take these things into school. Surely expensive items are safer left at home? Thanks for your call. Hope you're soon off sick leave and back at work. Sounds as if you're needed in that school! We've got a commercial break coming up but first let's go to Cheryl on line five. Hi, Cheryl.
Cheryl:	Yes, hi Don. I just had to give you a call this morning because I'm getting crosser with every call I hear.
Don:	What's got you so angry then Cheryl?

Cheryl: Well, I wish people would stop blaming the parents. I don't want my kids taking expensive things into school. But how do I stop them? They do it behind my back. Last week my youngest daughter, Lianne, took an expensive new toy into school and I got a call from the teacher later in the day to say it had been stolen!

Don: How did she take it in without you knowing, though Cheryl?

Cheryl: She just smuggled it into her bag without me knowing, Don. I'm a mother helping them get ready for school in the morning not a customs officer looking for smugglers.

Don: OK, I can tell that you feel strongly about this but why do they do it? Why do they take these things to school? Can you tell me that, Cheryl?

Cheryl: It's showing off, Don. They want to show the other kids that they have something expensive and better than the others have. That's all it is. Problem is the other kids then get jealous and nag their parents for the same things or else they steal from each other. I tell you, Don, it's not easy being a parent these days!

Don: OK, well that's Cheryl. I hope she feels less angry now she's had a chance to tell us all how she feels. I don't think she will be applying for a job as a customs officer, do you? Anyway, we've got one more call before the break and that's Phillip on line eight. Hi, Phillip.

Phillip: Hello Don. I'm fifteen and home sick today so I've been listening to your programme. I just wanted to tell you that our school won't let us bring expensive things into school, ever. And Don, I don't think kids should get expensive items from their parents unless they earn them by doing jobs and stuff. That's what I do.

Don: That sounds like a pretty sensible attitude to me, Phillip.

Phillip: Well, Don. It's stupid to take expensive or dangerous stuff into school anyway. It usually gets broken or stolen or lost. And some dangerous stuff just hurts other kids or influences the younger ones. It's stupid. Best to keep it at home and enjoy it when you get home or at weekends. If you want your mates to see it all just invite them round. I wouldn't take any of my expensive hi-fi equipment or computer stuff into school.

Don: OK, thanks, Phillip. He sounds as if he's got a lot of sense. We've got to take a break now but we'll be back with more of your calls in just a few minutes. This is Don Ratty on Talkback Radio 102.5fm and digital. Do kids get too much? Should they take expensive items into school to show off to their mates? Give us a call now.

Introductory questions the teacher may like to ask you about this topic before you start reading/acting this playscript:

1. Do your parents ever stop you taking certain things into school?
2. What things do you think should not be brought into school?
3. Has anyone ever brought an expensive item to school and had it stolen or broken? What happened? How did your parents react?
4. Anyone ever brought anything dangerous into school?
5. If you want to show your friends some of your things, how else can you do it without bringing things into school?

Questions about Scene 1:

1. How do both Abu and Phil react when they see Mike's new laptop?
2. Why do you think Phil's mother would never let him bring something like a laptop to school?
3. How did Abu's parents react when he once brought an old CD-player into school?
4. What are your feelings about Mike's relationship with his parents?

Questions on Scene 2:

1. If Naresh had to bring such a large amount of money to school, what should she have done with it to keep it safe in school?
2. Why did she bring it to school?
3. Why did her parents let her bring the money to school?
4. Who has Naresh inconvenienced? Who else is now involved because of her actions?

Questions on Scene 3:

1. Why do you think the teachers are so concerned about the magazine being in school?
2. What is their attitude towards the magazine?

Instant replay:

Paul: Well, I think it's disgusting how older kids try to influence the younger ones by showing them this kind of rubbish. They think they're being clever. They're just showing off, trying to act big.

What is your reaction to this teacher's comments?

4. What other items might older pupils bring into school that could be a negative influence on younger pupils?

5. Tricia says: "Their education began before they even entered the school grounds this morning!"

What does she mean?

Questions on Scene 4:

1. Is Mrs Singh correct to expect the school to pay for the damage to her son's CD-player? Explain your thoughts.

2. Whose responsibility is it for such an item when it is brought into school?

3. What steps has Mr Andrews taken to put matters right? Is it his responsibility to do all this?

4. Why had Mrs Singh's son brought the expensive CD-player into school?

Questions on Scene 5:

1. What sort of pressure do Jenny's children put her under to buy them the latest things?

Instant replay:

Jenny: If they need something for school then of course we make sure they have it but some of the things these other kids get given amazes me, it really does, Don. When my kids see those things they want them too! So what can you do?

Don: You can say no, Jenny, that's what you can do! I think some parents have lost the word "No" from their vocabulary!

Give your thoughts on Jenny's question and on Don's reply.

1. Who do you think is responsible for pupils bringing expensive, dangerous or other unwanted items into school? The pupils? The school? The parents?

2. What do you think of Cheryl's views?

3. Give your views on Phillip's final comments.

4. If you had been a caller to Don's phone-in, what points would you have made to him?

Playing
Up
Again

Script 5

"Let's Skip Lessons"

This play script looks at the problems and difficulties that can occur if pupils decide not to turn up to lessons during the school day.

Actors/cast required for playscript 5

*This play has (11) reading parts.

After each scene there are a number of questions to answer.

- Your teacher may decide that you should write down your answers instead of answering them aloud in class.

- Your teacher may decide that you should read the play right through first and then read it a second time, but this time answering the questions at the end of each scene before continuing.

- Decide who is to play each part.

- If you are chosen to play the part, think about how you will play the character and the voice/accent you might use.

- Will you be sulky? Enthusiastic? Sarcastic? Think of the tone of voice you might use.

- If you are performing it in front of the class or in assembly, what might you be doing? Where might you be standing or sitting?

Cast: Played by:

Nyonya Gahir   (boy pupil)   ....

Mrs Gahir   (mum)   ....

Sean Turner   (his mate)   ....

Teachers   **Georgina Fuller**   ....

Bob Leyton   ....

School Secretary **Mrs Morris**   ....

Bike Store Assistant   ....

Phone-in Host   **Don Ratty**   ....

Callers   **Kathy** (female)   ....

Azzat (male)   ....

Nadine (female)   ....

SCENE 1 – *In the school corridor just before lunch*

(The lesson is over and two pupils are standing at their lockers in the corridor)

Sean:	At last the morning's over. I'm starving. I really can't face maths this afternoon.
Nyonya:	I'm hungry too. That last lesson seemed to go on for ever. Still, it's lunchtime now and then we've got that maths test this afternoon. Did you learn for it?
Sean:	No way! Besides, we're not going to be here.
Nyonya:	What do you mean? Where are we going to be?
Sean:	Oh, wake up! We're not going to be in school this afternoon because we're going to check out the latest super bikes at Bike World in town. That's where we're going to be whilst the rest of them do their stupid maths test.
Nyonya:	No, Sean, I can't. You mustn't. Mum spent hours helping me learn for the test last night. I've got to do it.
Sean:	You get your mum to help you learn for tests? How un-cool is that? Oh well, if you haven't got the guts to live dangerously now and again I guess it's your loss. I'm going to have a great time. Is your mum coming into class to sit next to you while you do the test?
Nyonya:	Don't be stupid.
Sean:	Yeah, I know. You'd better do what your mum wants. After all, I'm only your best buddy. What does it matter if you let me down?
Nyonya:	Oh, don't say it like that. We're not allowed to skip lessons anyway. We might get stopped by the police in town and then we would be in real trouble.
Sean:	Will you listen to yourself! Do you like doing maths tests?
Nyonya:	You know I don't. Are we going to grab something to eat? I don't want to stand here all lunch hour arguing with you. I'm starving.
Sean:	OK, well let's go. We'll get some burgers in town and then we'll check out the bikes. They won't even notice we've gone. Come on. Stop making a drama out of it.

Nyonya:	What will I tell my mum when she asks how the maths test went?
Sean:	Oh, tell her you were in the toilets being sick. Tell her you had last minute nerves. Who cares? Come on. I'll meet you by the bus stop outside the gates. Nobody will even notice we've gone. I want to check out the latest Triumph Speed Triple. Looked awesome in this week's copy of Bike News and they've got one in the showroom in town. Come on, let's go.
Nyonya:	OK, but I hope you know what you're doing.

SCENE 2 – *In Bikeworld's showroom in town later that afternoon*

The shop assistant is standing in the background watching the two lads as they examine the bike.

Nyonya:	But you'd have to save up for years to buy a bike like that!
Sean:	I've got my weekend job, remember. Look at its body. Look at those cans!
Nyonya:	Yes, but you spend all the money the same day you get it.
Sean:	Well, I'll save it in future. Stop being so negative.
Nyonya:	Hang on. The assistant's coming over.

The assistant walks towards them, smiling falsely.

Assistant:	Beautiful bike that one. We've had a lot of interest in it. But shouldn't you two lads be in school this afternoon?
Sean:	No we get a double free period on Wednesday afternoons.
Assistant:	Which school is that, then?
Nyonya:	Oh, you wouldn't know it. It's not in this area.
Assistant:	So you're able to come in to town to shop during your free periods?
Sean:	Yeah. We've got a new headteacher. She's really young and tries out new ideas like that. It's a sort of flexitime. You choose when you want to be in school. The kids like it.
Assistant:	Yes, I'll bet they do!

Nyonya:	Yeah, it reduces congestion on the buses.
Assistant:	OK, that's fine. Just checking. We can't be too careful. We get truancy patrols checking around the stores these days.
Nyonya:	You do? What happens if they catch kids out of school?
Assistant:	You really want to know what happens?

(Nyonya is looking scared and nervous. The assistant notices this)

Assistant:	Well, they have large, fierce dogs with them that they use to round up the kids and get them into the black van.
Sean:	What happens then?
Assistant:	Then they take them straight to court and sentence them. Kids last week were sent to prison for twenty-five years.
Nyonya:	*(trembling)* Twenty-five years?
Assistant:	Do you want to look at some of the specs on these bikes, then?
Nyonya:	Oh is that the time? No, we'd better get going actually.
Sean:	Yeah, we've got a really important maths test. Really got to go. Can't miss that. Love maths tests.
Assistant:	But I thought you said . . . ?

(The two boys run off out of the store towards the bus stop)

SCENE 3 – *In the school office*

The school secretary, Mrs Morris, takes a phone call.

Mrs Morris:	Good afternoon, Monks Terrace School. May I help you?
Mrs Gahir:	Oh, yes, I hope so. It's Nyonya Gahir's mother. He's got a maths test this afternoon and I've just found his pencil case and maths equipment in the kitchen where he left it all last night. Could you get a message to him please? I can bring it in for him if he wants me to.
Mrs Morris:	Just a moment, Mrs Gahir. I'm just looking at the attendance computer and according to that, your son is absent this afternoon. He was here this morning but has not registered for afternoon classes.

Mrs Gahir: But where is he? There must be some mistake with your computer. This test is very important to him. We spent hours last night revising for it in the kitchen.

Mrs Morris: I'm sorry. We've no idea where he is. He didn't bring a doctor's note or dentist appointment card. You didn't ring us to say he was ill. If he had felt sick in school he would have gone to the medical room and they would have informed me in the office.

Mrs Gahir: Well, now I'm beginning to get worried. I thought he was safe in school. He could be anywhere. He may have been in an accident. Anything could have happened to him.

Mrs Morris: I'm sure there must be a simple explanation for this. I shouldn't worry Mrs Gahir. I'm sure he's fine. I'll speak to his Head of Year and ask her to check.

Mrs Gahir: Oh, thank you ever so much. Could you let me know when he turns up please? It's just that I tend to worry and get myself upset at times like this. I'd hate anything bad to have happened to him.

Mrs Morris: Yes, I'll phone you straight away. And don't get too upset. It will all be OK, I'm sure.

SCENE 4 – *In the staffroom some minutes later*

The secretary, Mrs Morris, is speaking to some of the teachers.

Mrs Morris: Well, his mother sounded most concerned.

Bob Leyton: But he was in my class just before lunch. I remember speaking to him and reminding him not to rock back on his chair. He'll break the legs off one of these days. Can't be any good for his back muscles either.

Georgina Fuller: He attended my Home Economics class this morning too. He almost burnt the potatoes he was cooking. Mind you, I've spoken to the maintenance department twice already this week about the strength of the gas flame. It's far too fierce. Someone will burn themselves one of these days. I seem to have the opposite trouble at home. Takes me ages to cook a decent meal.

Mrs Morris: Well, he's not in the medical room. I've just checked again.

Bob: I'll take a wander into his class. See if anyone knows anything about it.

Georgina:	Who is his best friend?
Bob:	Oh, yes, it's young Sean Turner. He'll be bound to know. I'll pop into his class and see Sean. I think they have a maths test at the moment so I'll try not to disturb them too much.
Mrs Morris:	It's worrying when we can't find them.
Georgina:	Yes, I get very worried if they're not where they are supposed to be. No wonder Mrs Gahir sounded so worried. Let me know how you get on, Bob.

SCENE 5 – *At the Gahir home later that day*

Nyonya is speaking with his mother in the sitting room

Mum:	Whatever were you thinking of? I can't believe you would do such a thing. I really can't.
Nyonya:	Sorry, mum. But the school wouldn't have known if you hadn't phoned up.
Mum:	Oh, so now it's all my fault is it? I only phoned the school because I found your pencil case and maths equipment in the kitchen and thought you would like me to bring it into school for you for the maths test. So now I'm to blame for you skipping school am I? You don't know how worried and upset I have been this afternoon. I thought you were injured somewhere.
Nyonya:	Sorry, mum. No I'm the one to blame I know that. You were only trying to help me.
Mum:	When you're in school I know you are safe and there are adults around who have your well being at heart. If you're hanging around the town centre instead of being in school, anything could happen to you.
Nyonya:	Yeah, but in school the teachers don't really care about you.
Mum:	Oh yes they do. Your maths teacher phoned me later. Really worried he was. Nobody knew where you were or if you were safe. You could have been abducted or had a road accident. You could have been lying on a stretcher in accident and emergency. How would we know?
Nyonya:	Oh, don't be stupid, mum.

Mum: It's not being stupid, Nyonya. If you had been hit by a car whilst skipping school, how would I have known? You've caused me and your teachers a very anxious afternoon. I thought you had more sense, I really did. And what about all that work we did for your maths test last night? I thought you cared about your work and wanted to get good qualifications to get a good job? But then you go and do this!

Nyonya: Sorry, mum. But Sean said it would be OK and no-one would notice we'd gone into town.

Mum: Oh, and you are too weak to resist his stupid ideas, are you? Can't you think for yourself? Can't you think about the possible consequences of your actions and the effect on other people, too?

Nyonya: Sorry, mum. I'm sorry about the maths test, too.

Mum: It's a good job your maths teacher cares about you. He's going to stay late tomorrow afternoon to let you and your silly friend do the test then. You see? People do care about what happens to you. So stop letting them and yourself down.

Nyonya: You mean I can still take the maths test?

Mum: Thanks to your teacher giving up his own time. Now phone your friend, Sean and let him know the good news.

Nyonya: Oh, he'll be speechless, mum. He really will!

SCENE 6 – *Talkback Radio 102.5fm and digital*

Don Ratty: Right well, we're into our final hour of the morning phone in and we're talking about school truancy this morning. Give us a call now on 777942 and give us your thoughts. The Government says that when kids skip school they often take part in crime instead of being behind their desks in school. Have you ever truanted? Have your kids ever truanted? What do you think of how the government is trying to stop it? Are they being tough enough? Are they getting too tough? Give us a call now. I'm Don Ratty and let's go straight to the caller on line ten and that's Nadine. Good morning, Nadine.

Nadine: Hi, Don.

Don: What do you want to tell us, Nadine?

Nadine:	Well, Don, my neighbour's daughter hardly ever goes into school. She spends most of her day listening to loud music. We can hear it from the kitchen here. Now they've been told her mother may go to prison because her daughter doesn't go into school.
Don:	And what do you think of that?
Nadine:	Well, I actually agree with it. I think parents have to be responsible for their kids. They have to make sure they go into school. I give mine a good breakfast before sending them off each morning.
Don:	But after your kids have had that breakfast of yours, Nadine, how can you guarantee they actually turn up or actually go into their lessons?
Nadine:	Yes, I know what you mean, Don. But the school would tell me if they didn't.
Don:	Right. We've got to move on. Thanks for your call. Let's go to line seventeen and speak to Azzat. Morning, Azzat. I believe your wife is a teacher?
Azzat:	That's right, Don. Her school has this arrangement to phone parents at work or at home and tell them if their child isn't in school.
Don:	Sounds a helpful idea. Does it work?
Azzat:	Yes, well, it has cut down the numbers of kids missing school because they know their parents will be informed straight away. My wife says they take a roll call in every lesson, too.
Don:	Well, if a kid's stupid enough to miss school and waste their only chance of a valuable education, why should I be bothered?
Azzat:	Because, Don, whilst they are skipping school, they may be breaking into your car!
Don:	Suddenly, I am bothered; you're right, Azzat!
Azzat:	Thought you would be, Don. Good talking with you. I really enjoy your show.
Don:	Thanks, Azzat. This is Don Ratty on Talkback Radio 102.5fm and digital. We've got time for one more caller before the break and that's Kathy who's fourteen. Not in school today Kathy?
Kathy:	Couldn't be bothered, Don. Thought I'd skip school and listen to your show instead.

Don: Do your parents know you've skipped school today?

Kathy: I live with my dad. He doesn't care if I go in or not.

Don: What about all the education you're missing? How will you get good qualifications? You'll want to get a good job one day won't you?

Kathy: I don't know what I want to do anyway.

Don: Your dad may get prosecuted or even sent to prison if you don't attend school. Why don't you attend, Kathy? What's the reason?

Kathy: It's just boring. The lessons are just boring and the teachers don't care about you anyway. They're probably glad I don't bother going in.

Don: So what do you do instead?

Kathy: I watch TV, listen to CDs or go into town with my mates.

Don: Have they skipped school, too?

Kathy: Some of them. So what? I'm not going to tell you their names.

Don: It's OK, I don't want to know who they are. But you realise you face a lot of risks out there unsupervised all day instead of being in school? Anything could happen to you.

Kathy: I can take care of myself.

Don: OK, well that's Kathy telling us why she skips school. What are your thoughts? Tell us what you think of Kathy and her mates skipping school. Remember the number: it's 777942 and we'll be right back after this break.

Introductory questions the teacher may like to ask you about this topic before you start reading/acting this playscript:

1. What is the law about attending school?
2. Why do you think some kids decide to skip school? What types of things do they get up to whilst skipping school?
3. What are some of the dangers they could face whilst skipping school?
4. What is the procedure at your school if you need to miss any part of the school day for a particular reason?

Questions about Scene 1:

1. What reasons were there why Nyonya should stay in school and not do what his friend, Sean, wanted him to do?
2. How did Sean try to persuade his friend to skip school that afternoon?
3. Give an example of how Sean uses sarcasm to persuade his friend.
4. What do you think of Nyonya's decision to do what his friend wanted?

Questions on Scene 2:

1. As part of their deception, what lies do the two boys tell?
2. Why do you think the store assistant was suspicious of the two lads?
3. How does the assistant cleverly convince them to abandon their shopping afternoon?

Questions on Scene 3:

1. Why does Mrs Gahir telephone her son's school?
2. How does she react when she is informed that her son is absent from school?
3. For what reasons is it all right for a pupil to miss school during term time?

Questions about Scene 4:

1. How do the teachers react when the secretary tells them about the telephone call from Nyonya's mother?

Questions on Scene 5:

1. To start with in this scene, whom does Nyonya blame?
2. His mother explains her fears about what could have happened to her son whilst he was out of school. What were they?

Instant replay:

Nyonya: Sorry, mum. But Sean said it would be OK and no-one would notice we'd gone into town.

Mum: Oh, and you are too weak to resist his stupid ideas, are you? Can't you think for yourself? Can't you think about the possible consequences of your actions and the effect on other people, too?

List what you think are all the possible consequences of his actions. Then list the other people who were also affected by how he behaved.

Questions on Scene 6:

1. During the radio phone-in, Nadine said her neighbour may go to prison. What do you think of the idea of jailing the parents of truants? Look at points for and against such action.

Instant replay:

Nadine: Well, I actually agree with it. I think parents have to be responsible for their kids. They have to make sure they go into school. I give mine a good breakfast before sending them off each morning.

Don: But after your kids have had that breakfast of yours, Nadine, how can you guarantee they actually turn up or actually go into their lessons?

Explain how responsibility and trust are both part of this.

3. Do you agree with the checks they carry out at Azzat's wife's school? Explain

4. Don says: "Well, if a kid's stupid enough to miss school and waste their only chance of a valuable education, why should I be bothered?" Why does he change his mind?

5. What is your view of Kathy's attitude? How would you persuade someone like her to turn up at school for lessons each day?

Playing Up Again

Script 6

"It's Making Me Angry"

This play script looks at some of the ways we might reduce our anger in situations when we are getting annoyed.

It looks at the effect of anger and violence and how it might be reduced.

Actors/cast required for playscript 6

*This play has (**12**) reading parts.

After each scene there are a number of questions to answer.

- Your teacher may decide that you should write down your answers instead of answering them aloud in class.

- Your teacher may decide that you should read the play right through first and then read it a second time, but this time answering the questions at the end of each scene before continuing.

- Decide who is to play each part.

- If you are chosen to play the part, think about how you will play the character and the voice/accent you might use.

- Will you be sulky? Enthusiastic? Sarcastic? Think of the tone of voice you might use.

- If you are performing it in front of the class or in assembly, what might you be doing? Where might you be standing or sitting?

Cast:		Played by:
Mother		....
Father		....
Ella	(daughter)	....
Teachers	**Mr Holmes**	....
	Mrs Gupta	....
	Mr Carter	....
Pupils	**Robert** (boy)	....
	Sanjay (boy)	....
Don Ratty		....
Phone-in Callers	**Adrian** (male)	....
	Anil (male)	....
	Debbie (female)	....
		....

SCENE 1 – *In the kitchen of a family's home*

(Ella is having a heated discussion with her father.)

Ella: But why can't I stay out till the rest of them do? Their parents are letting them stay out till midnight but you want me back here by ten thirty.

Father: I don't care what their parents are doing. It really does not concern me at all. You are our daughter and you will be back here by ten thirty.

Ella: Well, how come you let Mark stay out till gone midnight? You never make a fuss about it with him.

Father: Your brother is older than you are and he doesn't have school the next day. He goes out to work and is old enough to make his own decisions.

Ella: Oh, well, stuff the lot of you!

(She throws a glass tumbler into the sink. It smashes and she runs out of the room. She passes her mother who is about to enter the kitchen.)

Mother: Hey, slow down! What's going on? Hey, where's she running off to so upset?

Father: *(shouts after his daughter)* Come back here young lady! Spoilt little madam. Wait till I get hold of you!

Ella: *(shouting back from upstairs)* I'm sick of being treated like a kid all the time. I'm fourteen not six!

Father: Then start acting like it for a change. And you can come down here and clean up this broken glass in the kitchen.

Mother: She will have to learn to control that temper of hers.

Ella: Drop dead both of you! You make me sick. Other parents listen to their kids and let them do what they want. Well, I'm staying out until my mates all go home and that's that!

Father: Well, don't bother coming back here. The house will be locked at 10.30.

Ella: Stuff the house! I don't give a damn what you both think. All parents make me sick. I can't wait to leave home! Why can't you be like Gemma's parents? I hate you!

In the kitchen of a family's home.
(Ella is having a discussion with her father.)

Ella: But why can't I stay out till the rest of them do? Their parents are letting them stay out till midnight but you want me back here by ten thirty.

Father: I realise they are able to stay out until twelve but we would like you back here by 10.30 please. We care about you and would worry if you were out at such a late hour.

Ella: I know that you want me back by 10.30 and I realise that it's because you care about me but I'm going to feel really stupid and embarrassed telling all my mates I have to leave early.

Father: I understand what you're saying and I realise how you feel but have you considered that we get very anxious about you being out so late at night? Particularly as it's a school day next day.

Ella: I hear what you're saying, dad, but I also know that everyone else is going to think I'm really stupid having to come home so early. They'll all laugh at me and tomorrow the whole school will see me as a sad joke.

Mother: I get worried, Ella, when it gets late and you're still out.

Ella: Mum, I understand how you feel but I'd like you and dad to reconsider.

Father: We know it's not the best decision as far as you can see but your mother and I have discussed the situation and we would like you home by 10.30, Ella. I know you understand our point of view.

Ella: Dad, I'm sure we can talk this through and try to reach a compromise.

Mother: I know you feel disappointed, love, but we ask you to be in by 10.30 because we get worried about your safety. We would never forgive ourselves if anything happened to you.

Ella: Mum, I appreciate what you're saying and I accept the point you're making but let's see if we can work out an arrangement that suits us all.

Father:	Tell you what, I'll give Amanda's parents a call and see if her parents can pick you all up together at eleven fifteen and bring you home.
Ella:	Thanks, dad. I know that when we all talk things through together calmly we usually find the best answer. Mum, can I borrow your silver watch to wear? You know, the cool, modern one with the weird face?
Mother:	I think I feel another of those family discussions coming on. Here we go again!
Father:	I think you could be right!

SCENE 3 – *In the school playground after two boys have been fighting*

One boy, Sanjay, is still on the ground; the other is brushing himself down as the teacher speaks to them.

Mr Carter:	Well, I hope you're both satisfied with the chaos you've both caused out here in the yard this lunchtime?
Robert:	Wasn't my fault. He had a go at me so I hit him. I give as good as I get!
Mr Carter:	Oh that's a great attitude, that is. So the whole school gets to gather round and watch the free show and cheer you on?
Sanjay:	*(begins to stand up)* Wasn't my fault. We didn't ask them to watch.
Mr Carter:	So, was it worth it?
Robert:	Don't ask me.
Mr Carter:	I am asking you. You choose to get involved in a nasty fight in your lunch hour. The whole school stands around chanting and cheering and I'm asking you to tell me what it solved.
Robert:	Well, he started it.
Mr Carter:	That's not what I asked you.
Sanjay:	Well, I'll get him back anyway.
Mr Carter:	I don't think so, Sanjay.
Sanjay:	But he insulted my parents!

Mr Carter: Is that what all this is about? Robert, I want you to go and wait outside my office. I think you and I need to talk. *(Robert exits)*

Mr Carter: Well, Sanjay?

Sanjay: I don't have to stand here and take it when he insults my parents' backgrounds. I don't insult his family.

Mr Carter: So laying a punch on him gets to the root of the problem does it? Oh that's very clever. I thought you had more sense quite frankly.

Sanjay: What would you have done then?

Mr Carter: There are other ways you could have dealt with it.

Sanjay: Like what for example?

Mr Carter: You could have come and told me for a start.

Sanjay: Oh yes, he'd have liked that. Me running straight to a teacher with my problems.

Mr Carter: Yes maybe. But you have to get to the root of the problem and find out why he chooses to insult your parents. Being violent in the school yard doesn't solve anything except get both of you into trouble. Anyway go along and sit in your form room. I'll talk to both of you more after lunch. As if I didn't have enough to keep me occupied. Off you go.

SCENE 4 –   *In the staffroom as the end of lunch approaches*

Mr Holmes: So he just punched him?

Mr Carter: Yes he did. Meanwhile the whole calm of the school is shattered as they all stand around chanting and cheering them on. Must be great to have a job where you can relax at lunch time!

Mr Holmes: Where are they now?

Mr Carter: I've separated them for the rest of the lunch hour and I'll see them both in my office later.

Mr Holmes: Why do they always see a violent response as a first response? Whatever is the matter with them?

Mrs Gupta: Come off it, Clive. Every time they turn on their TV sets they see other males solving their problems by using violence. It shouldn't surprise any of us when they behave in the same way here in school, surely?

Mr Carter: She's right, Clive. In soap operas, movies and other TV dramas the screen is full of guys solving conflict by being violent towards each other. These kids are watching all that and behaving in the same way. They all have televisions in their bedrooms nowadays.

Mrs Gupta: Exactly. What sort of message does it all send out to teenage boys?

Mr Holmes: I suppose you're right. It's the same on news bulletins, isn't it? They always seem to focus on conflicts being solved by more violence.

Mrs Gupta: Well, my youngest daughter was sitting watching cartoons the other morning and even the cartoons were full of characters punching, kicking and throwing people off the roof!

Mr Carter: Yes, but that's only fantasy violence.

Mrs Gupta: Yes, but they see a cartoon character who is thrown off the roof just jump up and continue the fight! They think violence is acceptable and then they behave just the same!

Mr Holmes: And we wonder why these kids get in trouble for fighting in school.

Mr Carter: Anyway, the bell's about to ring and I'd better go and see them both in my office. I'll talk to them and explain that it's only by talking through problems and conflict that both sides actually get to solve their problems.

Mr Holmes: I heard you are up for the Nobel Peace Prize this year, Gareth?

Mrs Gupta: Well, I'm beginning to think that teaching these kids the skills of conflict resolution is as important as teaching them maths and science!

Mr Carter: Has either of you seen my coffee cup? Wouldn't mind a quick cuppa before I referee round two.

Mr Holmes: There's only one clean one left.

Mr Carter: OK, I'll fight you for it!

Don Ratty: It's twenty-five minutes past ten on 102.5fm and digital. I'm Don Ratty and this morning we're asking for your views on violence in our society. John Merchant is here with the latest world news at the top of the hour but now let's go to line twelve where Debbie is waiting to talk with us. Morning, Debbie. Sun shining in your part of the country?

Debbie: No, it's been pouring down for hours, Don.

Don: I should stay in and listen to us if I were you. What point do you want to make, Debbie?

Debbie: Well, I was contacted by the school the other day. They phoned me at home and told me that my youngest son was involved in an incident where he really lost his temper in class. Well, last night I was reading about "e-numbers" and how they can affect your temper.

Don: Can they make a child more violent?

Debbie: Well, Don, it seems they can. It seems that lots of fizzy drinks, sweets and other foods that kids eat have got high levels of e-numbers in them that make them angry, lose their temper and contribute to hyperactive behaviour.

Don: Well, I'm sure lots of parents listening will want their kids to avoid those. Problem is, Debbie, lots of schools sell those foods and drinks in their school tuck shops and canteens. Anyway, we must move on and take another caller. Let's go to Anil who is on line four. Morning, Anil. I believe you've recently witnessed a violent attack?

Anil: Yes I certainly did, Don. It really scared me, too, I can tell you. We were travelling along on an A-road and there were two cars in front of us travelling really close together. They were too close. It looked as if they were almost glued together. Well, Don, the first one braked suddenly and the one behind went straight into him. The second driver then got out of his car and went up and punched the driver in front. It was pretty scary to watch. They didn't discuss anything; he just punched him.

Don: Yes violence in road rage is a nasty new aspect of life, isn't it? I'm lucky. I've never experienced it, Anil.

Anil: Well, what amazed me is they didn't even discuss what happened. Their first impulse was to be violent. Luckily a police car was nearby and the officers calmed them down.

Don: If only people would think first and talk through their problems. Anil, thanks for your call, mate. This is Talkback Radio, I'm Don Ratty and you can call us now on 777942. And we've got Adrian calling us on line seven. Morning, Adrian.

Adrian: Hi, Don. I'd just like to let you know what happened last weekend when I took my three kids to the football.

Don: Even football matches can be pretty violent places these days, Adrian, can't they? What happened, mate?

Adrian: Well, there was a punch up on the pitch and we saw people fighting in the crowd as well. The referee soon put a stop to the trouble on the pitch. He sent off the two players involved but the trouble in the crowd was getting too scary for me and I didn't want my children to see it so we left after the first half. I was disgusted.

Don: It's pretty sad when a father can't take his kids to the footie without witnessing violence. Do you think it was alcohol related, Adrian? It usually is.

Adrian: The trouble in the crowd certainly was. You could just tell. I shan't be going again until my kids are much older. Sad isn't it? Of course when the players themselves started fighting on the pitch it sends out all the wrong messages to young players, doesn't it, Don?

Don: I could not agree more, mate. Let's hope they put a stop to such anti-social behaviour and stop these louts getting into the game.

Adrian: Well, that's right, Don.

Don: Thanks for the call, Adrian. We've got to go I'm afraid. But we'll be back with more of your calls after this break.

Introductory questions the teacher may like to ask you about this topic before you start reading/acting this playscript:

1. Have you ever witnessed fights in the school yard? What are some of the reasons that can cause these fights?

2. Would you stand and watch? Would you go and get the teachers? Would you try to break up the fight?

3. How do such fights affect the atmosphere of the school when it's time to go back into class?

4. "Some cartoons are too violent and should be banned." Do you agree?

5. How is the fantasy violence of movies and cartoons different from the violence we see in TV News programmes?

6. What sort of things can make you angry enough to want to fight or be violent?

Questions about Scene 1:

1. Why does Ella lose her temper?

2. Comment on this statement: "Losing her temper only makes her parents more determined not to let her have her own way."

3. Comment on how both Ella and her parents handled this conflict.

4. "Why can't you be like Gemma's parents" says Ella. What do you think she means by that?

Questions on Scene 2:

1. How does this scene differ from the first scene?

2. What feelings are expressed this time by the various characters?

3. What are the main points Ella makes in favour of being allowed to stay out until her friends have to come back?

4. What are the main points her parents make about why they want her back earlier?

5. How is a compromise reached?

6. Do you think this scene is a realistic example of how to handle conflict in a more diplomatic, less explosive manner? Explain.

Questions on Scene 3:

1. List all the consequences of the fight.

2. Mr Carter tells Sanjay there are other ways he could have dealt with the problem without resorting to violence. Give your own ideas of how else he could have dealt with it.

Questions on Scene 4:

Instant Replay:

Mr Holmes: Why do they always see a violent response as a first response? Whatever is the matter with them?

Mrs Gupta: Come off it, Clive. Every time they turn on their TV sets they see other males solving their problems by using violence. It shouldn't surprise any of us when they behave in the same way here in school, surely?

1 Give examples from television and film that you have seen, that could influence children to behave in a violent way.
2 The media may be one factor that can influence children to be violent. What other factors could there be?
3 Mr Holmes says: "I heard you are up for the Nobel Peace Prize this year, Gareth?" He is being sarcastic. What is the Nobel Peace Prize? Use the internet or your library resource centre to research some of the winners of this prize over the past fifteen years and why they won it.
4 Many members of the school gathered round and chanted and cheered as the two boys fought in the playground. What effect might this then have as they all begin their lessons after lunch?

Instant Replay:

Mrs Gupta: Well, I'm beginning to think that teaching these kids the skills of conflict resolution is as important as teaching them maths and science!

Do you agree with her? Explain.

Questions on Scene 5:

1. Debbie made a point about how certain food and drink can cause people to lose their temper. Research more about e-numbers and how some food and drink can affect behaviour. What are your views on this?
2. Should schools ban fizzy drinks and certain popular foods from their premises in case they cause pupils to be violent? What are your views?
3. Anil phoned in to tell about a case of road rage. Have you ever seen an example of this whilst travelling? How else could such disputes be dealt with without resorting to violence?
4. What do you think should be done about violence at football matches? Why do you think it occurs?

Drama:

Students may also like to invent a follow up scene to the play from where it left off after scene 5.

Playing Up Again

Script 7

"The Public Is Watching You"

This play script looks at some of the behaviour that can make school trips and excursions difficult.

It looks at the views of the public, the pupils and the staff.

Actors/cast required for playscript 7

*This play has (14) reading parts.

After each scene there are a number of questions to answer.

- Your teacher may decide that you should write down your answers instead of answering them aloud in class.

- Your teacher may decide that you should read the play right through first and then read it a second time, but this time answering the questions at the end of each scene before continuing.

- Decide who is to play each part.

- If you are chosen to play the part, think about how you will play the character and the voice/accent you might use.

- Will you be sulky? Enthusiastic? Sarcastic? Think of the tone of voice you might use.

- If you are performing it in front of the class or in assembly, what might you be doing? Where might you be standing or sitting?

Cast: Played by:

Mr Cooper   (Science teacher)   ....

Mrs Yeni   (Maths teacher)   ....

Bob Sterling   (Geography teacher)   ....

Head Teacher   ....

Pupils   **Tanya** (girl)   ....

                Eilish (girl)   ....

                Martin (boy)   ....

Members of the public

                Lady 1   ....

                Lady 2   ....

Radio phone-in host **Don Ratty**   ....

Male callers   **Khaya**   ....

Female callers **Brenda**   ....

                Joan   ....

                Anuja   ....

Mr Cooper: Now they want to know if they can take their mobile phones on the coach in case it breaks down and they have to phone home!

Mrs Yeni: Is it worth all this work just to take one class on a trip to the zoo? You've been rushing round for the last week getting all this organised. I hope they appreciate it.

Bob Sterling: You watch out. They'll want to bring home a tiger cub or baby python next!

Mr Cooper: Well, they're really looking forward to this trip.

Mrs Yeni: I'm sure they are. It gets them out of school for a day, doesn't it? But look at all the organisation you've had to do.

Mr Cooper: Yes, but the trip is based on sound educational reasons.

Bob Sterling: Keep telling yourself that and you'll believe it!

Mrs Yeni: Have you spoken to them about their behaviour? You don't want them showing you up in public.

Bob Sterling: Nor destroying the extremely high reputation of this wonderful place of academic learning.

Mr Cooper: Can you two be serious for just a moment? If you really want to know, yes I've spoken to them about the standard of behaviour I shall expect of them.

Bob Sterling: Oh, let me guess. No spitting, no chewing, no hanging out of the coach windows in a tunnel; don't swear at the zoo staff; don't throw your litter into the giraffe's cage; don't wander off and don't make rude signs behind the monkeys' backs. Some monkeys really take offence to that! Can't imagine why! Something like that was it?

Mrs Yeni: Sounds like a pretty fair list of demands to me!

Mr Cooper: It's easy for you two to make fun. But I have to remind them about all that because the public will be watching them. They will be representing our school in public.

Mrs Yeni: Heaven help us all then! I'd better start applying for other jobs in case we get closed down.

Bob Sterling: I remember a trip I organised about a hundred years ago. Some child kept picking its nose in the museum and before we returned to school a member of the public had already telephoned the Headteacher to complain!

Mrs Yeni: Well, I don't envy you taking that class to the zoo tomorrow, Paul.

Mr Cooper: Didn't you look at the staff roster for tomorrow afternoon? You're down on the list to come with us and help supervise them! I hope you like zoos!

(Mrs Yeni looks crushed and Bob bursts out laughing.)

SCENE 2 – *On the coach to the zoo*

Tanya: Bus driver looks a bit miserable, Miss.

Mrs Yeni: He probably does a lot of these school trips.

Martin: How much longer is the journey, Miss? I feel a bit sick.

Eilish: Can we eat our packed lunches now, Miss? I'm starving.

Mrs Yeni: Another few minutes and we'll be there. It's just down the end of this next road, I think.

Tanya: I haven't got a ticket to get in, Miss.

Mrs Yeni: Don't worry, Mr Cooper has all the tickets.

Martin: I don't know why we weren't allowed to bring our mobiles. My mum wanted me to phone her when we arrived there to let her know I was safe.

Tanya: Liar! You said you wanted to chat to your girlfriend.

Martin: No I did not!

Mrs Yeni: Anyway, you'll just have to use a public telephone when we get inside the zoo.

Mr Cooper: *(via the coach microphone. Coughs into it to test it first.)*
Right, everyone. Listen please! The driver is about to stop the coach. We have to park just around the corner from the zoo entrance. Now when the coach stops I want you all to check that you haven't left any litter on board and then get off in an orderly and calm way. Line up in twos on the pavement so I can count you all. After all, we don't want to lose anybody.

Eilish: Who's got the packed lunches, miss?

Mrs Yeni: Don't worry. Mr Cooper has them and will give them out when we get inside the zoo. OK, now lead off from the front. Sensibly, Karen please. Ali I said from the front. Don't push! I don't want bruises on the back of my ankles. You have to wait years for surgery nowadays.

(Pupils leave the coach and line up noisily on the pavement. Two elderly ladies are standing at the bus stop talking. We can now hear their conversation)

Lady 1: Yes, you are right. Look how untidy some of them look.

Lady 2: I remember when I was a girl at school. Our teacher, Miss Broad, would never have let us wear our school clothes like that. I used to be scared to death of her.

Lady 1: Look at that one chewing! Look! Look!

Lady 2: School kids nowadays don't know how to behave properly, do they? Especially in public.

Lady 1: I blame their parents and teachers. They don't teach them manners anymore. Did you know that?

Lady 2: Look at those two punching each other. The one on the right looks as if he's a right little toughy. He's got an earring in his ear.

Lady 1: They shouldn't let them come to school looking like that.

Lady 2: Oh, wait a minute. The teacher is walking up to them.

Lady 1: The teacher looks as young as they are. She won't stop them.

Lady 2: Wait a minute. They've stopped fighting.

Lady 1: I should think so, too. Dreadful behaviour in public.

Lady 2: I know which school they're from. It's near where my son lives. I recognise the school uniform.

Lady 1: Yes, but look at that girl on the end of the line. She doesn't care about how she wears her school clothes. She's got her school shirt hanging out. Looks as if it could do with a good ironing, too.

Lady 2: Look at that. The lad at the front of the queue just threw his chewing gum down on the pavement. I don't know why teachers take them out in public these days when they behave like that.

Lady 1:	It's an easy day and a break for the teachers, I suppose.
Lady 2:	Here, where are you going?
Lady 1:	Just popping into this phone box. There's an important call I just have to make. Won't be long.

SCENE 3 – *At the zoo*

Mr Cooper:	No, don't wander off there yet. Let's all sit down on the grass for a moment. I want to talk to you all.
Eilish:	Can we have our sandwiches now, please, Miss?
Mrs Yeni:	Yes, Mr Cooper will give them out to you whilst you all listen carefully to me.
Martin:	Have we behaved all right so far, Miss?
Mrs Yeni:	Of course, I wouldn't expect anything less from you. Remember what I said, though. When we walk around the zoo I want us all to keep together and not go wandering off alone.
Tanya:	But Miss, can't we go to the souvenir shop? I want to get my mum a postcard.
Eilish:	What's the point of that? You'll be seeing her in a few hours!
Mrs Yeni:	No, that's fine. Mr Cooper's planned for us all to go to the souvenir shop before we get on the coach and head back to school.
Martin:	Sir, I'm going to really enjoy looking around the zoo. I've never been here before.
Mr Cooper:	Well, I'm glad to hear that. But you will tuck in your shirt before we go wandering around, won't you, Martin?
Martin:	But Sir, I like wearing it like this. We're not in school anyway, are we Sir? So it doesn't matter does it?
Mr Cooper:	Yes, but you're representing our school in public. The public is watching us. I don't want them to think we don't teach you manners or how to dress properly.
Martin:	Sorry, Sir.
Mr Cooper:	OK then. Eat your sandwiches and then we'll start our tour of the zoo. We'll go to the reptile house first.

Tanya:	Oh, Eilish will feel at home there, Sir.
Mrs Yeni:	Was that chewing gum you just threw down onto the grass?
Tanya:	Ah, yes miss.
Mrs Yeni:	Well pick it up and place it in the bin over there. We don't want a member of the public sitting on your dirty chewing gum and then phoning the school to complain about your behaviour. Right, where's my sandwich, Mr Cooper? Beef and pickle I think it was. OK, who's got it?

SCENE 4 –   *Headteacher's office*

(The Headteacher is on the telephone speaking to a member of the public who is phoning him from a public telephone box.)

Headteacher:	Yes? This is the Headteacher speaking. Yes . . . oh, I see. . . Yes, I appreciate your taking the time to telephone and tell me. What exactly were they doing as they lined up outside the coach? . . . I see . . . I see Would you like to give me your name? . . . OK. Right . . . Her shirt was what? . . . I see . . . Yes, I see . . . He did what with his chewing gum? Oh, I see . . . Really? Yes, I understand . . . I see. No, of course I will Yes, of course. I shall do that as soon as they return to school later this afternoon. . . Oh, I agree. We insist upon our pupils behaving well at all times in public . . . Yes, thank you and once again I appreciate your taking the time to find a telephone box to phone me . . . Yes, goodbye.

SCENE 5 –   *The Phone-in: Talkback Radio 102.5fm and digital*

Don Ratty:	Yes and you're listening to the morning phone-in here on Talkback Radio 105.2 fm and digital. We're talking this morning about how pupils behave in public. Do you ever watch in horror as pupils climb onto the bus in the afternoon? Have you ever heard pupils using language in public at which even a bricklayer would blush? Have you ever been in an art gallery when it's suddenly been invaded by a tribe of art loving invaders from the local school? Give us a call with your experiences and thoughts on 777942. I'm Don Ratty and this is Brenda on line five. Morning, Brenda.
Brenda:	Morning, Don. You made me laugh just then when you mentioned school kids storming into an art gallery. My husband and I were in the borough museum the other afternoon. We'd had a quiet lunch in their cafeteria and then we were wandering round looking at the exhibits.
Don:	Anything particularly catch your eye?

Brenda:	Well, Don, after a few minutes a party of school kids arrived with their teachers. Absolute mayhem suddenly broke loose. They started shouting out and racing around the place. We left after a few minutes.
Don:	Well, Brenda, what was their teacher doing to keep them in line, then?
Brenda:	Don, the teachers hardly looked much older than the kids were. They let them touch the exhibits, even when there were signs saying "Do Not Touch". But, Don, the language some of them were using! I would never allow my own kids to speak like that. There were lots of visitors in the museum that afternoon and they don't want to hear school kids using language like that! I felt embarrassed.
Don:	Did they have any worksheets with them or anything to focus on?
Brenda:	Oh, don't get me wrong, Don. Some of them were well behaved and were obviously finding answers for their worksheets. It was just the minority who let down the others. They let down their school, Don. I saw some museum staff having a word with one of the teachers. He didn't look too pleased, I can tell you!
Don:	OK, Brenda. Thanks for your call. We must move on and we've got Khaya on line ten. What point do you want to make, Khaya?
Khaya:	Well, Don, you want us to phone in with what we think about school kids and their behaviour in public is that right, Don?
Don:	Yes, that's our phone in topic this morning. Go ahead Khaya, you're on the air.
Khaya:	Well, I was in the theatre the other afternoon to see a matinee performance of a Shakespeare play. There were mostly elderly pensioners in the audience but just in front of where I was sitting was a class of pupils from the local school. I think they must have been studying the play for their exams.
Don:	Oh, yes, I remember doing a Shakespearean play when I went to school. "Romeo and Juliet" I think it was. Anyway, their behaviour was pretty rotten was it, Khaya?
Khaya:	Not at all, Don. I was very impressed by them. But the play was ruined for me because of the rustling of sweet papers and whispering throughout the performance.
Don:	But I thought you said the pupils' behaviour was good?

Khaya: Oh, yes, Don, it was excellent. It was the elderly pensioners who ruined it for me. They were eating from bags of sweets and rustling their sweet papers and constantly talking and making comments to one another. I had to ask one lady to be quiet because I just couldn't hear the actors' words.

Don: That is interesting, Khaya. So the kids from the school behaved well? It's good to hear that.

Khaya: Oh yes, definitely. I even went and told their teacher how impressed I was by their behaviour. And such good manners, too.

Don: What else annoyed you about the behaviour of the audience then?

Khaya: Well, many of them were late back after the interval and made such a noise getting back to their seats and disturbed everyone else. I think they had stayed too long in the bar or in the toilet. They set a poor example to the school pupils, I can tell you.

Don: Well, it's good to hear that some schools teach their pupils how to behave when out in public. Thanks for the call, Khaya. Ah, Shakespeare. I remember it well! This is Don Ratty on Talkback Radio 105.2 fm and digital and it's a quarter to twelve. We have Joan on line nine. Thanks for taking the time to call us, Joan. I believe you live on the bus route to the local school, Joan, is that right?

Joan: That's right. There's a bus stop right outside our house, Don.

Don: And what sort of things do you see going on?

Joan: Well, Don, I don't know where to start.

Don: I take it you're not impressed with the school kids who use your bus stop, Joan?

Joan: It's frightening, Don. The litter they leave there and the language they use. I've phoned the school many times about it, but it keeps on happening.

Don: So they don't represent their school well in public, Joan?

Joan: They certainly do not. They have their shirts hanging out and the girls are smoking. Some of them have thrown beer cans over my front hedge onto my lawn. My husband spends hours grooming that lawn. It's immaculate, Don. It's his pride and joy since he had to give up work with his bad veins.

Don:	So he's not too pleased to find cans and litter thrown over it, I suppose?
Joan:	It really upsets him, Don. The other day kids were spitting on the pavement right outside our front path. Well our Sarah brings her youngest in the afternoons. She's only three years old and I don't want her falling into that. It breeds germs doesn't it, Don? Filthy habit. I'll bet their parents would be horrified if they saw how their kids were behaving in public going to and from school.
Don:	Joan we've got to try and fit in one more caller. Thanks for ringing in and I hope your husband's lawn looks in top shape this morning. Right, our final caller is Anuja. Hi, Anuja. I believe you run the local shop at the end of your road?
Anuja:	Well my husband does but I often help serve in the shop with him.
Don:	I guess you have local school pupils to serve in the afternoons?
Anuja:	Well, that's right, Don and most of them are well dressed and very polite.
Don:	Oh that's refreshing to hear. Particularly after the previous caller.
Anuja:	Oh, yes. They have good manners and some even hold the door open for adults when they are leaving or help them with their heavy bags.
Don:	What about when they ask to buy from you? Do they use "please" and "thank you"?
Anuja:	The majority does, yes. You occasionally get the odd few who forget but most of them have very good manners.
Don:	OK, well, that's Anuja with a positive call to end the phone in this morning. Thanks for the call. Don't forget, if you still want to give us your views on how school pupils behave in public you can email us at: don@talkradio.co.uk News and weather coming next at the top of the hour. This is Don Ratty. I'll see you all tomorrow at ten.

Introductory questions the teacher may like to ask you about this topic before you start reading/acting this playscript:

1. Do you think pupils behave well when they are out in public?

2. Can you think of examples when you've seen pupils behave badly in public? What happened?

3. What impression do you think the public has of the behaviour of school pupils generally? Why do you think they have this impression?

4. Why do you think schools organise school trips?

5. Have the ones you've been on gone smoothly? What happened?

6. What do you think is involved in organising a school trip?

Questions about Scene 1:

1. Why do you think Mr Cooper does not want his pupils to take mobile phones on the school trip to the zoo?

2. Can you think of reasons in favour of them taking mobile phones?

3. What is Mrs Yeni's attitude towards school trips?

4. How would you describe Bob Sterling's attitude to school trips?

Instant replay:

Mr Cooper: Can you two be serious for just a moment? If you really want to know, yes I've spoken to them about the standard of behaviour I shall expect of them.

Bob Sterling: Oh, let me guess. No spitting, no chewing, no hanging out of the coach windows in a tunnel; don't swear at the zoo staff; don't throw your litter into the giraffe's cage; don't wander off and don't make rude signs behind the monkeys' backs. Some monkeys really take offence to that! Something like that was it?

Mrs Yeni: Sounds like a pretty fair list of demands to me!

*If you had been Mr Cooper, what would you include in your serious list of things to remind the pupils about before they go on the trip and the standard of behaviour you would expect of them on a school trip to the zoo?

5. How do you think Mrs Yeni feels when she discovers that she is to help supervise the trip?

Questions on Scene 2:

1. What were some of the things the pupils were nagging their teachers about during the coach ride?

2. Why did Mr Cooper want the pupils to line up in twos when they left the coach?

3. Why does Mrs Yeni want pupils at the front to leave the coach before the ones at the back?

4. What are some of the things the two lady onlookers disapprove of?

5. What do you think of their views?

6. Why do you think Lady 1 goes to the telephone box?

Questions on Scene 3:

1. At the zoo, why does Mrs Yeni ask them not to go wandering off?

2. What two aspects of their behaviour did their teachers remind them about in this scene?

Questions on Scene 4:

1. Who do you think was speaking to the Headteacher?

2. How do you think the Headteacher is feeling whilst listening to the person?

3. What do you think the Headteacher promises to do when the pupils return to school that afternoon?

4. What do you think are some of the things the caller is complaining about to the Headteacher?

5: Drama: You may like to write and act out a scene that follows Scene four. What happens when the pupils return to school?

Questions on Scene 5:

1. Give some examples of the pupils' poor behaviour in the museum.

2. What poor behaviour does Khaya tell Don about?

3. What does Khaya think of the pupils' behaviour at the theatre?

4. Why is Joan not pleased with how the pupils behave outside her house?

5. What are some of the good ways in which pupils behave in Anuja's shop?

Playing Up Again

Script 8

"Late Again"

This play script looks at the effect of lateness to class and how it can lead to problems later in life such as lateness to work or to important appointments.

Actors/cast required for playscript 8

*This play has (20) reading parts.

After each scene there are a number of questions to answer.

- Your teacher may decide that you should write down your answers instead of answering them aloud in class.
- Your teacher may decide that you should read the play right through first and then read it a second time, but this time answering the questions at the end of each scene before continuing.
- Decide who is to play each part.
- If you are chosen to play the part, think about how you will play the character and the voice/ accent you might use.
- Will you be sulky? Enthusiastic? Sarcastic? Think of the tone of voice you might use.
- If you are performing it in front of the class or in assembly, what might you be doing? Where might you be standing or sitting?

Cast: Played by:

Mr Sidhu   (Geography teacher)   ....

Mrs Layton   (Maths teacher)   ....

Shirley   (PE teacher)   ....

Tricia   (Class teacher)   ....

Pupils   **Angu** (girl)   ....

                Vicky (girl)   ....

                Cheryl (girl)   ....

                Marcus (boy)   ....

                Adam (boy)   ....

Mr Salisbury (employer)   ....

Daniel (employee)   ....

Mr Parsons (a father)   ....

Joanne (daughter)   ....

Richard (son)   ....

Taxi driver   ....

Radio phone-in host **Don Ratty**   ....

Male callers   **Peter**   ....

                Bernard   ....

Female callers **Omena**   ....

                Pauline   ....

SCENE 1 – *In the classroom*

Mr Sidhu: So please make sure you stick the map onto the left hand side of your next page. Is everyone clear about that? I don't want to have to repeat myself later.

(door opens)

Marcus: Sorry I'm late, Sir.

Mr Sidhu: All right, Marcus, take your seat quickly and quietly and get out your geography books please.

Angu: Shall I tell him what he's missed, Sir?

Mr Sidhu: No, it's all right, Angu. I'll go over it all again quickly. Right, everyone. Look this way. I'll just go over this again so we'll have you all looking this way. Quickly. Your attention here, please. Now, you have a map on a sheet I've given out to you. I'd like you to stick it onto . . .

(door opens)

Vicky: Sorry I'm late, Sir. My dad couldn't get his car to start.

Mr Sidhu: Well, you'll have to leave home earlier in future, won't you? Quickly take your seat and I'll go through everything again. Right everyone looking this way again please.

Adam: Sir, we know what we have to do. It gets boring if you keep going over everything again.

Vicky: But Sir, I don't know what I should be doing!

Adam: Then you shouldn't have been late.

Mr Sidhu: All right, you two. Less of that, thank you. You must all remember to arrive to class on time otherwise we're never going to complete all the work we have to cover. It wastes such a lot of valuable time having to stop and re-start the lessons for latecomers. The others get bored and I have to keep repeating myself. Now, let's try once more. OK? Everyone listening? Now take the printed maps on the sheets I've given you and stick them . . .

(knock at the door)

Mr Sidhu: Yes, what is it now? Oh, it's you, Mrs Layton.

Mrs Layton: Sorry to bother you Mr Sidhu. You all look very busy but I've just been hurrying these two along to your lesson. I found them in the cloak rooms and they didn't seem in any hurry to get to your class. I'm sure they'll be very keen to make up the work they've just missed. Anyway I shan't take up any more of your time.

Mr Sidhu: No, that's all right. Thank you very much Mrs Layton. You two, take your seats and get out your books. I'll be speaking with both of you later.

Adam: You're not going to go through everything again are you, Sir?

Mr Sidhu: Just a moment, Adam. Why were you two so late for this lesson?

Cheryl: Well, Sir. We know there's no point in coming on time because so many kids come late and you repeat all the instructions for the latecomers every time and that gets boring. So there's no point in coming on time. Do you see what I mean, Sir?

Mr Sidhu: So you thought you'd skip that part of my lesson and avoid getting bored? I hope everyone is able to hear that. Do you see the effect your lateness is having on everyone else? I want everyone of you here on time tomorrow. Without fail. Now, I'll try one more time. Get out the maps I have given you and stick them . . .

Marcus: *(yawns loudly)*

Mr Sidhu: Not getting bored, I hope, Marcus?

SCENE 2 – *Office of Rayner's Aerospace Limited*

Mr Salisbury: Yes, the door is open. Come in, Daniel.

Daniel: Morning, Mr Salisbury. You wanted to see me?

Mr Salisbury: Yes, Daniel. As you know, you've been with us for four months now and we've been pleased with how you've settled in. Your floor manager tells me you've been producing some very good work for the company.

Daniel: Thanks very much, Mr Salisbury.

Mr Salisbury: Unfortunately, I have to give you this.

Daniel: What is it Mr Salisbury?

Mr Salisbury: It's a written warning about your poor time-keeping. You get into work far too late each morning and you often return late from your lunch break. It won't do, you see? We have to employ people we can trust to be here on time and give us a fair day's work for a fair day's pay. Sound fair?

Daniel: Yes, and I'm really sorry about it all Mr Salisbury but it's difficult to find a car parking space.

Mr Salisbury: Then you'll have to leave home earlier. It's as simple as that. When you arrive late your colleagues have to cover for you and do work that you're supposed to be doing. We can't go on like that.

Daniel: I know, Mr Salisbury and I am trying to arrive earlier.

Mr Salisbury: Well, you'll just have to I'm afraid. Our company operates with every member of the team carrying out his or her clearly defined tasks. If you can't be here on time we'll just have to let you go, Daniel. That would be most unfortunate as you're a good worker otherwise, I think you'll agree?

Daniel: Yes and I love working here.

Mr Salisbury: I noticed in your final school report you showed us when we first offered you the job, that your Headteacher commented on your frequent lateness to class.

Daniel: But that was usually my dad's fault because we got stuck in traffic on the way in every morning.

Mr Salisbury: Well, you need to take responsibility for your own time-keeping and you have to start showing us you can be here on time, Daniel or you'll have to start looking for somewhere else to work. As I say, here's your first official written warning.

Daniel: I promise you I'll be here on time tomorrow Mr Salisbury.

SCENE 3 – *Outside a house in Myrtle Road*

Mr Parsons: Please don't sit on those suitcases, Joanne. You'll break the lock and then everything will spill out in the aircraft's hold. Some holiday that will be!

Joanne: Oh, I'm getting bored waiting here. Let's go back inside and sit down then.

Richard: Dad, we're going to miss our flight if the taxi doesn't arrive soon.

Joanne: You did remember to phone for one, I suppose?

Mr Parsons: Yes, I did. I stressed to them that we had a flight to catch as well.

Joanne: Why are we waiting out here? Can't we all go back inside the house and wait there?

Mr Parsons: No we can't. The moment the taxi arrives I want to put the cases straight into the boot and get going. There isn't a moment to spare now.

Richard: Well if he's not here in the next few minutes we're not going to make it and we might as well unpack and stay at home. The road to the airport gets really busy.

Mr Parsons: Give me your mobile, will you? I'll phone them and see what the delay is. There must be a pretty important reason why they're so late.

Joanne: Dad, he should have been here twenty minutes ago. Oh this is embarrassing. The whole street can see us standing outside with our cases.

Mr Parsons: Yes, hello? Look we ordered a taxi for 10.30 and it's now 10.50 and there's still no sign of it. We have a plane to catch at midday and we're going to miss it if you don't arrive soon. Yes…Parsons. P-A-R-S-O-N-S. Lever Street. Number 24.

Joanne: Dad, tell them we'll never use their taxi company again if we miss this flight.

Richard: Hang on, dad. He's here. I can see the taxi coming round the corner!

Mr Parsons: Oh it's OK, your taxi's here. Yes, OK, bye. Right now, quickly you two. Let's get the cases into the boot and we'll be off. Sunny Spain here we come!

Taxi Driver: Sorry I'm late, mate. Had to stop and deliver the wife to her mother's place first. They're going shopping together in town.

Joanne: We have a plane to catch and you're very late!

Richard: Oh come on, Dad. Let's get going.

Mr Parsons: This is no way to run a taxi company. You've not heard the last of this!

SCENE 4 – *The Staffroom*

Mr Sidhu: That's the second time this week she's been late to my geography lesson. I had to re-start the lesson three times with the others coming in late.

Shirley: Well, I shouldn't worry, Bob. If they can't be bothered to get here on time, why should we upset ourselves?

Mr Sidhu: But it's the other kids I feel sorry for. The ones who are on time and want to work. We've got a lot to get through this term. We have to complete the syllabus.

Shirley: I know what you mean. I was teaching a group in the gym the other day. I had just finished explaining all about a sequence of moves on the mats when three others turned up late so I had to go through it all again! I know exactly how annoying it can be.

Tricia: Oh, Bob. I'm putting my class reports together and I don't seem to have your geography reports for them?

Mr Sidhu: You don't? Are you sure?

Tricia: No. They were due in to me by yesterday afternoon. I want to finish putting them in order tonight at home and I can't do it if yours aren't there.

Shirley: What were you saying about lateness being annoying, Bob?

Mr Sidhu: Sorry, Tricia. I'll write them tonight. You'll have them first thing in the morning.

Tricia: That's no good, Bob. I'm going out tomorrow evening. I particularly planned to keep this evening free to finish them off. Now yours are late I'll have to cancel my evening out tomorrow and stay home and do them then.

Mr Sidhu: I'm so sorry to inconvenience you, Tricia. I'll work through my lunch hour now and write them for you. You'll have them before you go home tonight.

Shirley: I wonder where your class gets its lateness from, eh Bob?

SCENE 5 – *The Phone-in: Talkback radio 102.5fm & digital*

Don Ratty: It's eight minutes past ten on 102.5fm and digital. We're talking this morning about a report in this morning's papers which says that lateness costs the country millions of pounds a year. Are you a person who can never do anything on time? Have you been the victim of people who have let you down because they are always late? We want to hear your experiences. Call us now on 777942. I'm Don Ratty and our first caller this morning is Omena. Morning Omena.

Omena: Hi there Don. I listen to you every morning. I never miss a show.

Don: Great. Thanks. Hope you never tune in late? What can we do for you Omena?

Omena: Well, Don you could have been talking to a rich woman this morning but it all went wrong because someone was late.

Don: Sounds interesting. Tell me what happened, then.

Omena: Well, I entered a magazine competition last year and nobody got the right answer. Nobody at all. Except me. But I didn't win the prize money because the postman was a day late collecting the post from the local post box and it never reached them in time. I had my entry in the post box and it would have reached them the next day, the closing day, but the local postman was late collecting from the box and so I missed out on the prize.

Don: So you missed out not because you were late but because of someone else's poor time keeping?

Omena: That's right, Don. I think of it even today, every time I pass that post box. My life could have been so different.

Don: OK, Omena. Sorry to hear that but thanks for telling us your story and keep listening. We need listeners like you. Let's go to Peter who's on line twenty-seven. Morning, Peter. What's your experience of lateness?

Peter: Well, Don, I was building a new house for a local businessman. I'm a building contractor and we had to finish the work by the end of March last year to get the bonus payment.

Don: I suppose someone you employed was late completing their part of the work.

Peter: Absolutely right, Don. We hired a team of electricians under contract to do all the wiring throughout the house before we were about to finish off the final parts of the walls. Unfortunately they were two weeks late turning up for the job and that put us all behind schedule. We didn't complete it on time and never got our bonus payments. The new owner was devastated and said he'd never employ us again. Told everyone we weren't dependable.

Don: That's one sad series of events, Peter. All because someone was late for their part in it.

Peter: That's right, Don. That example of lateness proved very expensive for us.

Don: OK. It's the morning phone in. 777942 is the number to ring. I'm Don Ratty with you until midday today and we're talking about lateness. 777942 is the number to ring. Let's go to line 7 where Pauline is waiting to speak to us. Morning, Pauline.

Pauline: Good morning, Don. I'm one of your regular listeners.

Don: Good to hear from you, my love. I believe you had a visit to the theatre ruined recently, is that right?

Pauline: Well, you see, Don. We always get there early and settle into our seats. I go with the other members from the Ladies Guild. They usually have a good drama or sometimes a nice musical on there. Well, ten minutes after the play had started, some people arrived late. I think they were on a coach trip together to the theatre.

Don: I suppose they made a lot of noise getting to their seats and you all had to stand up to let them through? There isn't much space between the seats in the theatre is there, Pauline?

Pauline: Well you're right, Don. They were pushing their way through and rattling bags and coats and it totally spoiled the play for me I'm afraid. Even the actors on stage had to shout to be heard.

Don: I didn't think they let you in until the interval if you arrived late for the theatre?

Pauline: I know what you mean. But they let this group in and they ruined the evening for everyone.

Don: OK, Pauline. Let's hope your next trip with the Ladies Guild is a much happier evening out. Thanks for your call. This is Talkback radio, I'm Don Ratty and we've just got time to talk with Bernard. Morning, Bernard.

Bernard: Hi, Don. Look, I've been listening to all these folk phoning you and thought I'd ring up and have my say.

Don: Well, we're glad you could join us, Bernard. What do you want to tell us about lateness?

Bernard: Well, Don, I was on a one hour parking meter the other afternoon and my wife had to have her hair done. She's normally in there for about three quarters of an hour or just under. Well this particular day they were running very late.

Don: Oh dear, you're going to tell me you had a nasty shock when you got back to the car?

Bernard: That's right Don. A parking ticket sitting right across my windscreen. We were only five minutes late!

Don: And those five minutes cost you a parking fine.

Bernard: That's right, Don. If the hairdresser hadn't been running late we wouldn't have been late back to the car and would not have got that parking fine.

Don: It was good talking to you, Bernard. Did your wife's hair look good after her appointment?

Bernard: Terrific!

Don: OK, well thanks for the call. Right, if we don't finish there then the News and Weather is going to be late and then I'll be in trouble. We've got to go to a commercial break now and then to the news. I'll speak with you all after the sports headlines on Talkback Radio 102.5fm and digital. Back soon with more of your calls.

Introductory Questions (before reading the scripts):

1. Can you think of times when being late for something has led to problems for you? (in/out of school)

2. How many people here would often be late for school if their parents or guardians didn't wake them up and organise them in the morning? How could you start taking responsibility for this yourself?

3. Has anyone here ever had comments in their school reports about their lateness? How could this affect you if a future employer read it?

4. Can you think of how a situation has been totally changed or affected by something happening later than planned?

5. Lateness can often have a "ripple effect" like a stone in a pond. For example, if the wife of a bus driver is late getting up and she is unable to wake him on time, he'll be late to the depot. His bus is late going out and the pupils are late to school. The Headteacher's Assembly is then late starting and . . . etc . . . etc. Can you think of another example of this "ripple effect" because of lateness?

Questions about Scene 1:

1. Why does Adam say he is starting to get bored?

2. What are the reasons for some of the pupils' lateness to class?

3. How do you think Mr Sidhu feels when his pupils are so late to class?

Questions on Scene 2:

1. Why is Mr Salisbury unhappy with Daniel?

2. What reason does Daniel give for his lateness to work each day?

3. How does Daniel's lateness affect other workers in the company?

4. Why does Mr Salisbury mention Daniel's school report?

5. What excuse does Daniel make for his lateness when he was at school?

6. What may happen if Daniel continues to be late at Rayner's Aerospace Limited?

Questions on Scene 3:

1. Why does Mr Parsons not want them all to wait inside for the taxi?

2. Why is Joanne getting embarrassed?

3. Why is it so important that the taxi arrives on time?

4. What do you think of the taxi driver's excuse for his lateness?

5. How would you have felt if you had been in that family's situation?

Questions on Scene 4:

1. Why do the teachers say it is annoying if pupils come to class late?

2. How has Mr Sidhu inconvenienced Tricia?

3. What does Shirley mean by her sarcastic final remark?

Questions on Scene 5:

1. How had lateness caused Omena to lose money?

2. Why did Peter never receive his bonus payment?

3. How could theatre staff have prevented Pauline's evening from being ruined because of lateness?

4. What caused Bernard to receive a parking fine? How could it have been avoided?

Playing Up Again

Script 9

"Turn Off That Mobile"

This play script looks at some of the benefits and some of the problems created by pupils using mobile phones.

Actors/cast required for playscript 9

> *This play has (13) reading parts.

After each scene there are a number of questions to answer.

- Your teacher may decide that you should write down your answers instead of answering them aloud in class.
- Your teacher may decide that you should read the play right through first and then read it a second time, but this time answering the questions at the end of each scene before continuing.
- Decide who is to play each part.
- If you are chosen to play the part, think about how you will play the character and the voice/ accent you might use.
- Will you be sulky? Enthusiastic? Sarcastic? Think of the tone of voice you might use.
- If you are performing it in front of the class or in assembly, what might you be doing? Where might you be standing or sitting?

Cast:		Played by:
Teachers	**Mr Barnaby**	....
	Mrs Trent	....
	Mr Ansari	....
Pupils	**Carole** (girl)	....
	Dougie (boy)	....
Members of the Public	**Naisha** (girl)	....
	Paul (boy)	....
	Mum	....
Radio phone-in host	**Don Ratty**	....
Male callers	**Ali**	....
	Sam	....
Female callers	**Janet**	....
	Helen	....

SCENE 1 – *In the kitchen at home*

Mum: I'll have to pick you up early from school this afternoon if we are to reach the hospital in time. But we can only go if Grandad is able to have visitors. He may not be well enough after his operation. I'll phone the hospital at lunchtime and find out first.

Carole: But you'll have to let me know, Mum, if he is not well enough for us to visit so I don't have to leave lessons early.

Mum: Well, keep your mobile switched on and I can call you to let you know.

Carole: No, Mum. We're not allowed to have our mobiles switched on during class. The teachers go mad if we do.

Mum: Well this is an emergency. I'm sure they'll understand.

Carole: Do you think Grandad will pull through his operation all right?

Mum: I don't know, love. He's quite elderly but very strong for his age. This operation could really give him many extra years of quality life. You know the terrible pain he's been in lately.

Carole: Do you think he'll feel like seeing us this afternoon? He might take a few days to recover.

Mum: Well I think he will, but if the hospital tells me he's not really up to having visitors then I'll phone you on your mobile, OK?

Carole: What if the teachers don't let me use my mobile in class?

Mum: That's OK. I'll leave a message with the school secretary and she can pass it on to you in class. Don't worry.

Carole: OK but last week our science teacher confiscated Cheryl's mobile because she was texting someone during the lesson.

Mum: And I don't blame the teacher either. Cheryl should not be texting during the lesson. But you have a good reason to have your mobile switched on today, love, don't you?

SCENE 2 – *In the classroom*

Mr Barnaby: Make sure you all leave a space after your last piece of work so we can stick in the comments sheet. Have you all got that? *(Mobile ring tone is heard)* Whose phone is ringing now? You know the school rules about mobiles being switched on in class.

Dougie: Sorry, Sir. I forgot to turn it off…… It's off now, Sir.

Mr Barnaby: Yes, well make sure it stays off. It interrupts the lesson and disturbs people who are trying to work.

Carole: I keep mine switched off, don't I, Sir?

Dougie: It won't happen again, Sir.

Mr Barnaby: *(He walks up to Dougie, slowly)* Dougie, what are you doing now?

Dougie: Sir?

Mr Barnaby: You're sending a text message aren't you?

Dougie: Only a short one, Sir.

Mr Barnaby: Right, give me that mobile phone. I've had enough of this. How can you concentrate on my lesson when your mind is on a text message? There's a time and a place for everything. I'll keep this phone for now.

Dougie: Oh, Sir. When can I have it back?

Mr Barnaby: You may collect it from me at the end of the afternoon. Oh and I'll have your mobile as well, Carole. You may both collect them at the end of school. I'm not running the risk of any more mobiles being used and disturbing this lesson.

Carole: But, Sir. I wasn't using mine. And, Sir, my mum may be phoning me on my mobile because my grandad's had an operation.

Mr Barnaby: No I'm sorry. This is a classroom not a telephone exchange. I will not have pupils using their mobiles in my lesson. You both know the school rules on this.

Carole: But, Sir! She has to phone and let me know if she'll be picking me up to visit him after his operation. I need to know if I have to leave early to meet her.

Mr Barnaby: Well, I'm sorry. Give me the phone. I'm sure your mother will phone the school office and let the secretary know if she needs to contact you urgently. Now…..where were we? Oh yes. Let's all write the titles under the maps.

Carole: *(whispers)* Thanks a lot, Dougie. That was all your fault!

SCENE 3 – *In the Staffroom*

Mr Barnaby: It happened again in class this morning! Mobile rang. Totally disturbed my concentration. Next minute he's texting his mates! Another pupil said her mother was going to ring about her sick grandfather. They seem to totally depend on using these mobiles every moment of the day!

Mrs Trent: That's an old excuse about the sick grandfather. I've heard that one many times. Anyway, I think all mobiles should be left at home. They don't belong in a school. We can't expect our lessons to be disrupted constantly.

Mr Ansari: Yes, but some parents say they want their children to keep their phones on them for their own security.

Mr Barnaby: I can understand that, actually.

Mrs Trent: How were we able to come to school and cope without mobile phones when we were children growing up? We seemed to cope all right.

Mr Barnaby: Yes but it's a different world nowadays.

Mr Ansari: I saw one of the mothers driving into the school car park to pick up her child yesterday afternoon. She had a mobile telephone almost glued to her ear! It was a wonder she didn't knock anyone over whilst driving. How can she drive and concentrate on a telephone call at the same time?

Mrs Trent: It sets a very bad example to the pupils if you ask me. It's also illegal to use mobiles when you drive.

Mr Barnaby: I spent over an hour of my time helping one of my pupils to find his missing mobile phone. She thought it had been stolen. Latest model too. We searched all over the school. Even announced it in school assembly. I even spent fifteen minutes on the phone to her parents about it. They were blaming the school for her having lost it!

Mr Ansari: Did you find it?

Mr Barnaby: Oh, eventually. Someone else had hidden it under her PE clothes just to annoy her.

Mrs Trent:	It's all extra time we spend, unnecessarily looking for mobile phones like that when they go missing. As if we didn't have enough to do!

(Bell rings for next lesson)

Mr Ansari:	OK, well I must go. By the way, let me know if you want those two lottery tickets in the staff lottery, won't you?
Mrs Trent:	Oh, how kind of you! I'll give you a call on my mobile later.

SCENE 4 –   *In the Cinema*

Naisha:	*(whispering)* Great movie. Do you reckon she's going to find the body behind the door?
Paul:	*(whispering)* I don't know. Not scared are you?
Naisha:	*(whispering)* No way! Look, I think she's going to tell him the truth. Listen she's about to tell him.

(Someone's mobile phone rings in the audience)

Paul:	What did she say? Did she tell him the truth?
Naisha:	I don't know. I couldn't hear a word.
Paul:	Someone must have forgotten to turn off a mobile phone. How slack!
Naisha:	Now it's ruined the entire movie. Come on let's leave. No point in staying now.
Paul:	Some people just don't care about others, do they?

SCENE 5 –   *The Phone-in: Talkback radio 102.5fm and digital*

Don:	18 degree high expected today with a cool breeze from the south west. You're with Don Ratty on Talkback Radio 102.5fm and digital. We're taking your calls this morning about mobile phones. Do you like them or hate them? Useful or a real nuisance? Give us a call and tell us your story. Janet is on line ten. Morning, Janet. Are mobiles something you love or something you love to hate?
Janet:	Well, Don. I think they're very useful actually and I'm phoning you because I'm angry.
Don:	Yes, I can hear that, Janet. What's happened? Are they charging you too much to make your mobile calls?

Janet: No, it's not that, Don. My son goes to school and the school has told him he can't take his mobile to school. It's making me very cross because we bought it for him for security. He's got it with him as he travels to school on the bus each morning and if he's late home in the afternoon he phones us and tells us where he is.

Don: I suppose it stops you worrying about him and if he's OK?

Janet: Well, yes it does, Don. I know I can contact him at any time and if he ever gets into trouble he can give me a quick ring. How dare the school say he can't bring it to school with him!

Don: Well, let's look at it from their point of view, Janet. I suppose they don't want kids texting each other in lessons and ring tones going off in the middle of exams.

Janet: I understand that Don. But surely they can see a mother's point of view as well? A child's safety is so important, Don.

Don: OK, Janet, well maybe teachers will give us a call and give us their point of view. Thanks for the call. Nice talking with you. 777942 is the number to ring on the morning phone in and Ali has phoned us on line seventeen. Morning, Ali.

Ali: Don, I had to phone you today and tell you I was rescued in an emergency because I had a mobile phone with me.

Don: Sounds pretty dramatic, Ali. Tell us all what happened.

Ali: Well, Don. I was trapped in a locked warehouse after all the other workers had left and gone home for the weekend. I was working in a downstairs store room and lost track of time. When I came up they had all gone and I was trapped. I could not get out. I shouted and shouted but no-one lives near the warehouse and no one could hear me.

Don: So how long was it before you remembered your mobile phone?

Ali: It was an hour or two and then I remembered it was sitting on the table in the canteen upstairs. I had been using it at lunchtime. So I raced upstairs and telephoned the warehouse manager who came and unlocked the place for me.

Don: They can certainly come in useful can't they, Ali?

Ali: You mean warehouse managers, Don?

Don: I meant mobiles actually, Ali. Anyway, thanks for your call. We've got to move swiftly on and talk to Helen on line four. Morning, Helen. I believe you hate these mobile phones? Why is that?

Helen: Oh yes, hi Don. I love your show. I listen to it at coffee time every morning. Yes, I hate these mobiles. My son has suffered because of them.

Don: Tell us all about it, Helen.

Helen: Well, Don, I gave him a mobile for his own security when he's travelling to and from school. Anyway, after a while he started getting very unhappy and didn't want to go to school. It seems other kids were bullying him by using text messages to insult him and call him names. Can you believe it, Don? Bullying by using text messages!

Don: I can actually, Helen. I hope you went and told the school about it.

Helen: Well, yes I did. They were very supportive and we traced the calls to two older girls who had decided to torment my son. The school dealt with it very well. But wasn't that a horrible thing for those two girls to do, Don? It made him very unhappy at school for quite a while. I hate mobiles now.

Don: They say children can be very cruel, Helen. Glad to hear it's all cleared up now and glad to hear their text calls could be traced so easily. Right we can pack in one more quick call before we take a break so let's go straight to Sam on line twelve.

Sam: Don, hi. I think these mobiles are a damned nuisance.

Don: Why is that, Sam?

Sam: I was on a long train journey recently from one end of the country to the other. Every few minutes someone's mobile started ringing or someone started talking at the top of their voice on their mobile. Even at night it was hard to get any sleep with the damned things ringing.

Don: Sam, I have to cut you off there as we're coming up to the break, but you've made your point well. I guess we've all been annoyed by phones on train journeys. Don't know what the answer is though. We'll be back in just a few minutes. I'm Don Ratty and this is Talkback Radio. I'm with you till twelve. Give us a call from your mobile!

Introductory Questions (before you read the play scripts):

1. Hands up how many people have a mobile phone.

2. Have you ever used them in situations where people object to them? What were their reasons?

3. Give me three points in favour of mobile phones and three points against them.

4. Should they be allowed in schools?

5. Have you ever been in a situation where mobile phones have helped in an emergency?

Questions on Scene 1:

1. How else could Carole's mother let her know if they will be able to see her Grandfather without using the mobile?

2. Why is Carole not allowed to use her mobile in class?

3. What is your view on that school rule?

4. Should pupils be allowed to send text messages from class?

Questions on Scene 2:

1. Why is Mr Barnaby so cross about the use of mobiles in his class?

2. Is Mr Barnaby right to take the phones away until the end of the school day?

3. How do you think Carole feels when her phone is also taken away?

Questions on Scene 3:

1. What do you think of Mrs Trent's view that all mobiles should be left at home?

2. What do you think about drivers who use mobile phones in their cars?

3. According to Mr Barnaby, how can mobile phones cause a lot of extra work for teachers?

Questions on Scene 4:

1. Cinemas ask people to turn off their mobiles during the movie. What should happen if people still keep them switched on?

2. How did a mobile phone spoil the film for Naisha and Paul?

3. Would you allow mobile phones to be used in: a restaurant? In a church? On a train? On a bus? In a theatre?
   Explain your answer.

Questions on Scene 5:

1. If you were Janet, what would you say to convince the school you were right?

2. If you were the school, what would you say to convince Janet you were right?

3. Ali was saved in an emergency. Can you think of other examples of how mobiles have saved or could save lives?

4. Have you come across examples of cruel text messaging similar to what Helen is telling Don Ratty about?

Playing Up Again

Script 10

"I'm Telling You For Your Own Safety"

This play script looks at the problems caused when pupils fail to listen to instructions given for their own safety and the safety of others.

Actors/cast required for playscript 10

*This play has (15) reading parts.

After each scene there are a number of questions to answer.
- Your teacher may decide that you should write down your answers instead of answering them aloud in class.
- Your teacher may decide that you should read the play right through first and then read it a second time, but this time answering the questions at the end of each scene before continuing.
- Decide who is to play each part.
- If you are chosen to play the part, think about how you will play the character and the voice/ accent you might use.
- Will you be sulky? Enthusiastic? Sarcastic? Think of the tone of voice you might use.
- If you are performing it in front of the class or in assembly, what might you be doing? Where might you be standing or sitting?

Cast: Played by:

Pupils	**Jaska** (girl)	....
	Gary (boy)	....
Phillip	(boy)	....
Helal	(boy)	....
Mr Ansari	(male teacher)	....
Jack	(pupil)	....
Mr Bennet	(Deputy Head)	....
Darren	(pupil)	....
Tiffany	(pupil)	....
Bus Driver		....
Miss Symes	(teacher)	....
Radio phone-in host **Don Ratty**		....
Phone-in callers **Angela**		....
Dominic		....
Stuart		....

SCENE 1 – *In the school yard*

(Evacuation during a regular school fire practice.)

Gary: I didn't even hear the fire alarm just now.

Jaska: Shouldn't we be running? After all, if it were a real fire we'd want to get out quickly!

Phillip: Oh, come on. It's only a practice. It's not the real thing. It doesn't really matter.

Mr Ansari: Hey! You three! Stop talking and walk briskly to the fire assembly area!

Jaska: But Sir, it's only a practice. Nobody's going to get burned alive, are they?

Mr Ansari: You shouldn't be talking during any evacuation. We need you all to remain silent in case we have to communicate vital information to you en route. Certain escape routes may be blocked by fire and we have to instruct you to take other paths. We can't do that if you're all chatting with each other, can we?

Phillip: Yes, but Sir that's not going to happen during a practice is it?

Mr Ansari: We still need you to react in exactly the same way you would if it were a real fire.

Gary: Oh, you mean we should all be screaming, "Help! Save me. We're on fire! Help!"

Mr Ansari: No I do not. You think it's all a joke, don't you? If a fire were to break out in school we'd need you all to be silent and evacuate calmly. That's why it's important for you to practise it as realistically as possible. Now walk calmly and silently and listen out for any announcements from Mr Bennet.

Phillip: We're just approaching the assembly area now anyway, sir.

Mr Ansari: Yes so we are but you should have walked here without speaking. This is an important evacuation practice not a walk to the local chip shop.

Jaska: Can we go on a walk to the shops when everyone gets here, sir? I'm starving.

(The others laugh quietly)

Mr Ansari: No we cannot. We have to take a roll call of everyone present. Somebody may be trapped back in the fire and we'd have to go back in and rescue them.

Gary: But Sir, hello? There isn't a fire. This is pretend.

Phillip: What he means is that if it were a real fire, they'd take a roll call and then if someone were missing they'd have to go into the blazing building and rescue them. Oh, and then all the teachers would have their pictures in the local paper for being heroes, isn't that right, sir?

Mr Ansari: Just stand quietly, Phillip and wait for the Deputy to carry out the roll call. Anyway, Jaska, you've been told about how to behave during a fire evacuation every term since you've been at this school.

Gary: She just doesn't listen, does she sir?

SCENE 2 – *In the classroom*

Mr Ansari: Right, you can finish off that exercise for your homework tonight.

Jack: Is that as well as all the other work you set us, sir?

(Knock at the door. Deputy Head enters.)

Mr Bennet: Excuse me Mr Ansari. I'm sorry to disturb your lesson but would you mind if I had a word with your class?

Mr Ansari: I'm sure the class is always happy to hear from you, Mr Bennet. They're all yours. Right everyone look this way and give Mr Bennet your undivided attention. Tiffany, that means you as well.
Sorry, Mr Bennet.

Mr Bennet: I just wanted to remind you about how dangerous it is to hang around cars in the school car park. As you know, a girl was injured last week when a visitor reversed his car and did not notice her. You must stay away from the school car park. We've also been asked by the local bus company to remind you to stay on the pavement behind the green barrier when you're waiting for your bus outside the school gates in the afternoon. All these rules are there for your own safety. The trouble is, many of you don't listen to reminders like these until it's too late. Anyway, I'm sorry to interrupt your lesson, Mr Ansari. Do carry on.

(Mr Bennet exits)

Mr Ansari: I hope you were all listening to that. Yes, Darren?

Darren: Sir, what happens if a teacher asks you to help them carry something heavy to their car? Will we have to say no?

Jack: That's a stupid question.

Mr Ansari: No, Jack, he's perfectly entitled to ask a question without someone making comments like that. Well, Darren, that's different. You'd be in the car park for a specific reason to help a teacher. Mr Bennet is talking about pupils who hang around between cars just chatting and day-dreaming or those pupils who like to play games around cars.

Darren: I see. Thanks, sir.

Tiffany: You should know, Darren. Remember when your parents had to pay to repair Sir's car last year when you were skate-boarding around it and damaged it?

Darren: Yes but I didn't do it on purpose. Sir knows that, don't you sir?

Tiffany: Still meant your parents couldn't afford a holiday last year because they had to pay for the damage!

Mr Ansari: All right. All right. Let's not go over all that again. Just remember what Mr Bennet said. Don't hang around in the school car park and don't go in there at all unless you're there for a specific reason.

Jack: Sir, I reckon there must be about a million rules in this school.

Tiffany: They invent them just to annoy us most of the time.

Mr Ansari: I think you'll find that most of them are there to protect your safety, Tiffany. Anyway, I've given you your homework for tonight so that's about it for today. Now, can you give me a hand with this box of books and help me carry it across to my car please Darren?

Darren: What's it worth sir?

Jack: The car's worth even less since you damaged it last year!

SCENE 3 – *At the school bus*

Helal: What time do we have to be there, miss?

Miss Symes: The play starts at three o' clock, Helal.

(Two boys run towards the school bus)

Gary: Come on, quick. I want to grab a seat at the back!

Joanne: I'll be there before you!

Bus driver: Hey! Calm down. Slow down. You're not pushing and shoving your way onto my bus like that.

Miss Symes: Yes, I agree. Now remember what I said to you all about behaviour on the bus. I don't want to be ashamed of you all before we even set off.

Joanne: Sorry, Miss Symes. I just want to get going. This is a cool idea to go to the theatre. My parents never take me.

Bus driver: I'm not surprised if you behave like that.

Miss Symes: Right now, I want you all to line up sensibly so I can count you all as you get on board. Sorry driver. When they are all seated I'll have yet another word with them about their behaviour. One…two..three…

(She begins to count them on)

Bus driver: Could you make sure they wear their seat belts? We've just had them fitted in this bus. Oh and remind them not to put their arms out the window. I don't like the sight of blood on my windows.

Gary: Oh, how gross! He'll be telling us we can't breath or speak next! He's a miserable bus driver, isn't he?

Miss Symes: . . . twenty three . . . twenty four. That's everyone, driver. Robert's ill today. His mother phoned me this morning. He was so looking forward to this theatre trip.

Bus driver: Do you mind if I have a word with them over my microphone? It won't take me long and then we'll get going.

Miss Symes: Oh, yes, be my guest.

Gary: What now? He **is** going to tell us not to breath. I knew it.

Helal: Sshh! Let's hear what he has to tell us.

Bus driver:	One, two three, testing. Can you hear me at the back? Now, I've been on these school bus trips before and I know what to expect. I don't want any litter or rubbish left on my bus. You must all stay in your seats when the bus is moving and keep your seat belts fastened. And keep the noise down!
Gary:	I knew it! Anyone would think it was his personal bus.
Miss Symes:	Thank you driver. Well, everyone, we're ready to go now. Just a reminder from me not to disturb the driver while the bus is moving. He needs to concentrate. Oh and no making faces at passing motorists. Your scary faces could make them swerve. They've got enough to worry about. OK, I think we're ready to set off driver.
Joanne:	*(whispers)* Miss, he's a miserable driver. I thought this trip was going to be fun?
Miss Symes:	*(whispers)* It will be Joanne, don't worry. He's only doing his job.
Bus driver:	Oh and if anyone gets travel sick, don't sit behind me!
Miss Symes:	Helal, come back here and sit by Gary. Happy everyone?
Gary:	Oh, but Miss!

SCENE 4 – *In the staffroom*

Mr Ansari:	We tell them but they just don't listen, do they?
Mr Bennet:	Pass us that newspaper will you, Ali?
Miss Symes:	When I tell them about the safety procedure in the bus or about the safety issues in the gym or drama studio you can see their eyes glazing over.
Mr Ansari:	When you came into the class the other afternoon, Phil, and spoke to them about the safety aspects of playing around cars, I don't think any of them was listening. Next week they'll all be playing in the car park as usual.
Mr Bennet:	Yes, but if any of them was injured, the Health and Safety people would need to know we had covered all the safety procedures with them.
Mr Ansari:	I understand what you mean. In the science lab I have to go through lots of safety procedures before they can handle equipment or chemicals. It's for their own safety. When I first started teaching a few years ago a kid burnt himself on a naked flame during an experiment. I never want that to happen again.

Miss Symes: But it will because they don't listen. I think they think we just like nagging them and imposing unnecessary rules.

Mr Bennet: We do! Ah, the power, the power!

Mr Ansari: No, but seriously, in some of my lessons they have to wear goggles and protective clothing. They still say, "Oh, Sir, do we have to wear this? It's messing up my hair." Ah, the photocopier is free at last.

Mr Bennet: Still, it's natural for kids to think that. They must get sick and tired of all the rules everywhere.

(Mr Ansari is bending down and probing the inside of the photocopier)

Miss Symes: Yes, but the rules are mostly based on safety reasons to protect them.

Mr Bennet: Hey, Ali, are you sure it's a good idea to be putting a knife inside a photocopier like that when it's switched on?

Mr Ansari: There seems to be some paper stuck inside wrapped around one of the drums. I've almost reached it.

Miss Symes: You'll electrocute yourself!

Mr Bennet: What's the telephone number of Health and Safety? I think I've just decided what the next staff training day will be about.

Miss Symes: But will they listen?

Mr Ansari: *(still struggling with a knife inside the photocopier)*
I've almost reached it . . . Has anyone got a match?

SCENE 5 – *The Phone-in: Talkback radio 102.5fm and digital*

Don Ratty: It's nineteen minutes to ten on 102.5fm and digital. We're talking this morning about whether our society has gone safety mad! A report in this morning's paper says we are in danger of grinding to a halt because safety procedures are stopping us from doing the simplest things anymore. What have you got to tell us about? Give us a call with your experiences on 777942. I'm Don Ratty. Next up this morning is Angela. Morning Angela; are you there?

Angela: Yes, Don, I'm here.

Don: What do you want to tell us, Angela?

Angela: Well, I'm a member of cabin crew on a local airline and I'm the one who gives the safety instructions before we set off.

Don: Oh it's you, is it? You're the one with a whistle between your teeth and a life jacket on. I've seen you waving your arms around! Do the passengers actually pay any attention to it?

Angela: Nobody ever seems to bother really. They all think it will never happen to them so they just don't follow the safety instructions at all. I think they're more interested in when the movie will start. We show some good ones!

Don: OK, well thanks for that, Angela. Let's hope they never need to use them in a real emergency. Right, let's go to our next caller on line sixteen and that's Dominic. Good morning, Dominic. You're an electrician, right?

Dominic: I sure am, Don and have been for over fifteen years. I'll tell you what, though, Don. You would not believe the reasons some people call me out.

Don: Try me.

Dominic: Well, they don't even bother to read the instructions on the appliances they use.

Don: Can you give me an example?

Dominic: Well, last week a woman phoned up because her electric iron had fused. When I got there she had failed to read some of the basic safety instruction. She had tried to pour water into the wrong compartment of her steam iron!

Don: She must have been pretty steamed up about it by the time you arrived, Dominic! Just goes to show that people don't really take any notice of basic safety information, do they? Thanks for your call. You're listening to me, Don Ratty on Talk-back Radio 102.5fm and digital. The time is twelve minutes to ten and our next caller is Stuart. I believe you're a fire fighter, Stuart?

Stuart: Yes, hi Don. I get called out to many emergencies as you can imagine. I get really annoyed because lots of them happen because so many members of the public don't read the safety instructions on the smoke alarms before they fit them.

Don: Oh, I've heard that many times. Stuart.

Stuart: I don't know why they bother fitting them if they don't follow the information about where to place them.

Don: But the instructions on them are fairly basic aren't they?

Stuart: Oh they are, but some people don't even put in a battery. I know that sounds hard to believe. Some even install the smoke alarms in parts of their homes where they won't be any use anyway. They have to read those instructions!

Don: Think you could be right about that, Stuart. Thanks for the call. We appreciate your taking the time to ring in. OK. It's the morning phone-in. 777942 is the number to ring. I'm Don Ratty with you until midday today. Back with more calls in just a moment at Talkback Radio 102.5fm and digital.

Introductory questions the teacher may like to ask you about this topic before you start reading/acting this playscript:

1. Has anyone here ever got into difficulty because they didn't read safety instructions before using something?

2. Which of your lessons here at school need to make pupils aware of safety issues in that lesson? (Perhaps because of equipment or tools you may have to use.)

3. Why do you think some people choose to ignore safety instructions or safety advice?

4. Which school rules at your school are based on reasons of safety?

5. Anyone here ever flown in an aircraft? Did you listen to the safety instructions before take-off?

Questions about Scene 1:

1. Why does Mr Ansari want the pupils to walk silently during the evacuation practice?

2. What signs are there that some of the pupils think the practice is just a joke and are not taking it seriously?

3. Why does a roll call have to be carried out in this sort of emergency practice?

Questions about Scene 2:

1. Why does Mr Bennet need to issue the reminder about car park safety?

2. Why does he need to issue the reminder about waiting for buses after school?

3. Mr Ansari later tells Jack that it is all right to be in the school car park for specific reasons. Can you think of three examples when it would be acceptable for a pupil to be in the school car park?

4. Why should Darren be particularly aware already about not playing near the staff cars?

Questions on Scene 3:

1. What things does the bus driver remind the pupils about?

2. Why does the teacher need to count the pupils each time they board the bus during a school trip?

3. Why do you think Miss Symes asks Helal to move and sit by Gary?

4. Do you think it is necessary for the teacher to remind pupils about all the safety concerns of the bus driver? Explain why you think that.

Questions on Scene 4:

1. What do the teachers think is the reaction of their pupils when they start reminding them about safety issues?

2. What indicates to you that even some of the teachers need to be reminded about safety issues?

3. Give one of the reasons a pupil gave about why they didn't want to wear protective clothing. If you were a teacher, how would you convince your pupils of the need to be aware of the safety issues?

Questions on Scene 5:

1. Can you think of examples nowadays where concerns about safety are restricting what children can do?

2. Why do you think passengers tend not to listen when Angela demonstrates the safety precautions on the aircraft?

3. Give examples of problems that may arise when people do not bother to read or listen to safety information.

4. Give examples of safety information in your school that pupils sometimes fail to remember or listen to.

5. What could be some terrible consequences if pupils do not listen to or read certain safety information?

Action replay:

Angela: Nobody ever seems to bother really. They all think it will never happen to them so they just don't follow the safety instructions at all. I think they're more interested in when the movie will start.

Can you suggest any ways for teachers to make safety information more interesting and more important in the eyes of pupils?

6. Can you think of examples at home and on public transport where there are important safety issues for people to remember?